GAY PLAYS
VOLUME TWO

Quaint Honour *by Roger Gellert*, Lies About Vietnam *by C.*
Timothy Mason, Cracks *by Martin Sherman*

Selected once again by playwright Michael Wilcox, this se̶c̶o̶n̶d̶
consists of two British and two American plays. In Roger Gellert's *Quaint Honour*,
homosexual relationships between schoolboys are depicted with vivid realism.
C.P. Taylor's *Lies About Vietnam* concerns two gay men trying to influence world
history and sort out basic matters in their own relationship at the same time. A
mysterious assassin is at large in Martin Sherman's *Cracks*, a play which is really about
. . . (a shot rings out) . . . ahhhh! Missed! Whilst *Bearclaw* by Timothy Mason details
the relationship between a gay native American and his dying patient. Each playwright
introduces his own play, except that *Lies About Vietnam* carries a preface by Michael
Wilcox, who also provides an introduction to the whole volume.

A METHUEN THEATREFILE

in series with

Other Spaces: New Theatre and the RSC
by Colin Chambers
The Improvised Play: The Work of Mike Leigh
by Paul Clements
The Plays of Edward Bond
by Tony Coult
**All Together Now: An Alternative View of
Theatre and the Community**
by Steve Gooch
Dario Fo: People's Court Jester
by Tony Mitchell
Peace Plays
(*The Tragedy of King Real* by Adrian Mitchell; *The Celebration of Kokura*
by Berta Freistadt; *Keeping Body and Soul Together* by Stephen Lowe;
Clam by Deborah Levy; *The Fence* by Common Ground)
Introduced and edited by Stephen Lowe
**How the Vote Was Won
and other suffragette plays**
(*How the Vote Was Won* by Cicely Hamilton and Christopher St John;
Votes for Women by Elizabeth Robins; *Lady Geraldine's Speech*
by Beatrice Harraden; *A Chat with Mrs Chicky* and
Miss Appleyard's Awakening by Evelyn Glover; *A Woman's Influence* by
Gertrude Jennings;
The Apple by Inez Bensusan)
Selected and introduced by Dale Spender and Carole Hayman
Plays by Women: Volume One
(*Vinegar Tom* by Caryl Churchill; *Dusa, Fish, Stas and Vi* by Pam Gems;
Tissue by Louise Page; *Aurora Leigh* by Michelene Wandor)
Introduced and edited by Michelene Wandor
Plays by Women: Volume Two
(*Rites* by Maureen Duffy; *Letters Home* by Rose Leiman Goldemberg;
Trafford Tanzi by Claire Luckham; *Find Me* by Olwen Wymark)
Introduced and edited by Michelene Wandor
Plays by Women: Volume Three
(*Aunt Mary* by Pam Gems; *Red Devils* by Debbie Horsfield;
Blood Relations by Sharon Pollock; *Time Pieces* by Lou Wakefield
and The Women's Theatre Group)
Introduced and edited by Michelene Wandor
Plays by Women: Volume Four
(*Objections to Sex and Violence* by Caryl Churchill;
Rose's Story by Grace Dayley; *Blood and Ice*
by Liz Lochhead; *Pinball* by Alison Lyssa)
Introduced and edited by Michelene Wandor
Gay Plays: Volume One
(*Submariners* by Tom McClenaghan; *The Green Bay Tree* by Mordaunt Shairp;
Passing By by Martin Sherman; *Accounts* by Michael Wilcox)
Introduced and edited by Michael Wilcox

GAY PLAYS

Volume Two

QUAINT HONOUR
by
Roger Gellert

LIES ABOUT VIETNAM
by
C.P. Taylor

BEARCLAW
by
Timothy Mason

CRACKS
by
Martin Sherman

Edited and introduced by
Michael Wilcox

A Methuen Theatrefile
Methuen . London and New York

A METHUEN PAPERBACK

This volume first published as a Methuen Paperback original in 1985 by
Methuen London Ltd, 11 New Fetter Lane, London EC4P 4EE
and Methuen Inc, 29 West 35th Street, New York, NY 10001, USA.

British Library Cataloguing in Publication Data

Gay plays. — (A Methuen theatre file)
   Vol. 2
   1. Homosexuality — Drama   2. English drama —
   20th century
   I. Wilcox, Michael, *1943-*   II. Gellert, Roger.
   Quaint honour
   822'.912'080353   PR1259.H6

   ISBN 0-413-59510-2

Printed in Great Britain by
Richard Clay (The Chaucer Press) Ltd,
Bungay, Suffolk

*PR
1259
.H65
.G39
V.2*

CAUTION

CONTENTS

INTRODUCTION

This second volume of *Gay Plays* contains two British and two American plays. As with *Volume One*, none of the plays is at present in print anywhere in the world, and three of them are published for the first time. As before, I have interpreted the notion of the 'Gay Play' as broadly as possible, and although homosexual, bisexual or trans-sexual characters are encountered in the pages of this anthology, the issues involved in the plays themselves go way beyond the sexual orientation of the characters.

Roger Gellert's own introduction to *Quaint Honour* provides an entertaining and candid account of the background of the play. First performed in 1958, at a time when all homosexual acts in Britain between males were a criminal offence, Roger Gellert depicts the sexual love of young boys in an open and daring manner. No wonder that Kenneth Tynan, in his *Observer* review, described the play as 'the most honest and informative play about homosexuality that has yet been performed in England'. The unpredictable flowering of youthful sexuality is still, in 1985, transformed by social and political attitudes into a thistle that is seldom grasped, except in the most sanitised (and therefore dishonest and unreal) and stereotyped manner by playwrights. 'The author of *Quaint Honour* sets out neither to apologise nor shock. This is how boys behave, he suggests. And his precise, well-observed play presents us with boys being lectured about the facts of life, boys being priggish and boys being Machiavellian, boys breaking each other like wild ponies. This is all so natural and true . . . and so rare in school literature . . . that the corollary that boys also make love to each other without ill effect is fed across the footlights and swallowed by the audience before they know what they are digesting.' Thus spoke the *Times Educational Supplement* reviewer in 1958, but stand in the corner the critic of the *Manchester Guardian* . . . 'honest play, but sickening . . .'

All British playwrights seem compelled to write at least one school play. *Lent* is my own contribution to the genre. Am I right in feeling that this is a peculiarly British obsession, especially with the ever present homo-erotic element lurking in the cloisters? I'd like to believe that Billy Bunter and his Greyfriars friends, and Jennings and Darbishire, and even the comic-strip Lord Snooty would all read *Quaint Honour* under the bedclothes in the 'dorm' with the greatest delight!

Lies About Vietnam dates from 1967, although it received its first performance in 1969 at the Traverse Theatre, Edinburgh, as part of a double bill, playing with another C.P. Taylor play, *Truth About Sarajevo*. *Lies About Vietnam* was written as a television play for Rediffusion Television. An internal memo from the 'Head of Programme Clearance' is reproduced in full later in this volume. It was leaked to Cecil Taylor at the time. 'There should be some warning to viewers of the homosexual theme so that the play can be avoided . . . The playing must be very discreet; as the men's situation is so clearly stated, there should be no touches of business in the production to emphasise it since any such would inevitably be regarded as tasteless.' (Thanks very much!) And this is about a play concerned with massive bombings, chemical attacks and massacres in Vietnam! As an example of the perversion of human values, that Internal Memo takes some beating. The play itself asks how people can hope to solve problems that challenge the survival of millions when they seem incapable of solving even their own intimate and most personal problems . . . a theme that was constantly explored in his plays and which reached its most devastating expression in C.P. Taylor's last great play, *Good*.

Taylor often had fun with people's names in his plays. I appear as a dumb police officer in *Bandits*. In *Lies About Vietnam*, Cyril is Cecil Taylor himself, Tom is Tom Pickard, the poet, and Frank Graham is a well-known Tyneside publisher. Part of Cecil's private work method involved imagining those around him were acting the parts of his characters. This helped to give them life in his mind's eye as he was hammering his typewriter. He wasn't trying to depict the real life models as they were in reality, but he imagined they were with him in his garden shed where he worked, enjoying a game of role playing and improvisation.

Taylor's concern with world history and American foreign policy, from the point of view of a Jew born in Glasgow and, in the mid-sixties, living in a caravan in Northumberland in extreme poverty, is contrasted in this collection with two American plays. *Bearclaw* by Timothy Mason depicts the relationship between an American – Indian nursing home orderly (gay) and an elderly patient (former history teacher and father). Writing in the eighties, Mason's gay character is presented without guilt, fear or apology. His 'native American' background and confident sense of identity combine to give him a great understanding of the dying Peter (a wonderful part for a senior artist). Toughness and delicacy, combined with a mastery of structure, introduce Mason as a natural dramatist. Doubtless, that 'Head of Programme Clearance' would have found Paul's unashamed confidence offensive and asked for his 'queerness' to be written out of the script.

Anyone attempting to analyse Martin Sherman's *Cracks* too closely is likely to get a bullet in the head. But before I leave the disintegrating world of *Cracks* well alone, let me pay tribute to its technical brilliance. Some plays seem to survive any sort of production one way or another. *Cracks* isn't among them. It requires virtuoso direction and performances, so many and so great are the risks Sherman takes. Behind it lies a vision of an endangered species in its final dance of death. The original manuscript should be bought without delay by the Natural History Museum.

As I write this, committal proceedings are underway in a British court against nine workers connected with *Gay's The Word* bookshop in London. Among the books seized by Customs Officers were novels by Tennessee Williams, Gore Vidal and Christopher Isherwood, and a medical book on AIDS. One of the Customs Officers was asked in court why a particular book, readily available elsewhere, had been detained. He replied that he might have detained the book 'because it had the name of a homosexual author on the cover.' British politicians who boast about freedom of speech, hang your heads in shame.

Michael Wilcox
July 1985

QUAINT HONOUR

'Homosexuality is not bad and, especially at school, may be positively good.'

Mary Warnock

ROGER GELLERT was born in Nottinghamshire in 1927 and has earned his living as a translator, reviewer, shopkeeper and broadcaster.

Quaint Honour was first presented at the Arts Theatre, London, on 1 May, 1958, with the following cast:

ROBERT HALLOWES	John Richmond
M.L. PARK	Philip Waddilove
J.V.H. TULLY	John Charlesworth
R.R. TURNER	Roderick McLaren
T.A.B. HAMILTON	Michael Caridia

Produced by Frank Dunlop
Settings by Paul Mayo

Characters

HALLOWES   A Housemaster, about 50, a humane man of faintly military appearance, and no fool. Understanding is his strong suit.

PARK   Head of House, 18, is small, square, very strong. Under a fierce exterior, a worried muscular Christian.

TULLY   A House Prefect, 18. A gangling figure, a handsome, unkempt head. Violent, sardonic and whimsical.

TURNER   A Junior, 14, a blue-eyed boy and a wag.

HAMILTON   A Junior, 14, a mild, innocent, studious boy, not ill-favoured, but dreary.

Scene

A Public School of the 1950s

Quaint Honour

This seems a strange little piece to me now. At the time I wrote it I was nuts about the theatre (which a year or two as a drama critic was soon to cure me of) but it had never occurred to me to write a play. I translated Corneille and Büchner; but I had no instinct for fiction, and couldn't have created a character to save my life.

I had been to a public school of early-Victorian vintage, geared largely to producing cannon-fodder for the Army and the Church. All it turned me into was a sceptic and a socialist, of a wettish kind. I very much doubt if it had anything to do with my being, as I gradually discovered, 'queer'. (That was the demeaning word we used then – though hardly worse than the fatuously wrist-flapping 'gay'.) Certainly no sexual experience of any kind can have contributed, since I had none. I was in a 'good' house (damn it), and as dankly virginal as the unawakened Hamilton of *Quaint Honour* – not at all the sort of cherub that arouses colourful thoughts in the minds of his elders.

A few years later I was talking over our school days with a friend who had been in the same house, and we achieved almost total recall of the Facts of Life talks routinely given to junior boys by our housemaster – a charming, humane and intelligent man with a striking resemblance to the American Bald Eagle. I decided to reshape it in slightly fictionalised form, as a comic scene involving two of his small charges, one already knowing more about sex than was good for him, and the other (like me) knowing almost nothing. It made a nice little sketch, but hardly the sort you could sell to an H.M. Tennent revue.

Shortly afterwards, another school contemporary – a rather malign character from another house – was showing me some of his old house photographs. In the back row of one group I saw with a shock of surprised recognition a fair-haired boy with an extraordinarily gentle and alluring face, like an innocent male 13-year-old Veronica Lake. I say surprised because I did remember him, and couldn't understand why, susceptible as I was to junior beauty, I hadn't fallen wildly in love with him. 'Oh, Crab,' said my host contemptuously, '*that* drip'. 'But he was beautiful,' I protested. 'Not the way I remember him,' said his housemate, showing me a later group in which I was unable to find the doe-eyed creature. He pointed to a bespectacled youth with the face of a whipped cur. 'Crab,' he said with satisfaction.

That night and on subsequent nights, in miserable dreams, the face of 'Crab' hovered weeping in front of me. I would awake shattered, powerless to undo a tragedy which I felt had long since happened: nothing dramatic, just the death of hope, the souring of a sweet nature by neglect. Why had *I* been such a drip, why hadn't I noticed him? If only I had been bold and bad enough to take him in hand and give him the love and reassurance he needed – instead of yearning for a stocky little scrum-half who needed me like a hole in the head.

As a kind of expiation – and exorcism – I took up the Facts of Life scene again and extended it into a play in which Hamilton finds a lover worthy of him: but a lover whom, in a sense, he outgrows. Once I had written the first draft, the miserable dreams stopped, and when eventually I dreamed of Hamilton again, he was calm and happy.

Although it deals with sex between consenting schoolboys – the only kind available in the circumstances, so that it can't seriously be regarded as 'deviant' – *Quaint Honour* was considered dynamite in 1958. The Swinging Sixties hadn't yet dawned, and despite all the evidence, children were still officially 'innocent': not in the moral sense in which they really are (until infected by adult guilt and calculation), but in the sense of pristine chastity, which even if it outlived the cradle would be of doubtful value. We hadn't, on the other hand, reached the poisonous hypocrisy of the present puritan backlash with, for instance, its brutal persecution of paedophiles: as gentle, harmless and indeed useful body of people, I should have thought, as exists in the community.

A 'club theatre' was the only hope, and Campbell Williams, maverick owner of the Arts Theatre, happily took a fancy to the play and defied the prudes. Peter Wood was to have directed, but got a better offer elsewhere, and the equally young Frank Dunlop shouldered the ticklish job. Our junior boys proved surprisingly easy to cast, and the hardest thing was to find a charismatic Tully. Various candidates came and went, either too rakish or too demure. At last, somewhat reluctantly, John Charlesworth came to audition, and we had our man. (It was, he said, one of the nastiest plays he had ever read, but the part was a juicy one.) Charlesworth, who started acting at 14, had briefly been the finest boy actor of his day – you can see him, for instance, in the 1950 film of *Tom Brown's Schooldays* where, as Tom's friend East, he decidedly outshines the star – and was now 23, a strikingly romantic figure, with a face that combined beauty and intelligence with a disturbing intensity. At this time he cultivated a smooth, wordly-wise manner, yet there was something slightly haunted about him. Nothing, though, that prepared us for his suicide only two years later, while rehearsing a leading role at the Birmingham Rep. The note he left spoke of letting people down – he had married in the meantime, but soon separated from his wife, and there were rumours of depression and debts. It was a wretched snuffing-out of what should have been a shining life. Perhaps a Tully was more vulnerable than a Hamilton.

The real-life Hamilton in due course married a Canadian girl and became a personnel manager in a computer firm. Park (my scrum-half) became a Squadron-Leader. Tully was not based on anyone in particular, though his Shakespearean rehearsal techniques (and nothing else!) evoke my Cambridge contemporary John Barton.

I have made some cuts and minor alterations to the text. At the time of writing, my theatrical god was John Whiting – a most unhelpful influence – which accounts for the mandarin quality of some of the dialogue, and for Tully's tendency to tirades (he was named after the orator Cicero). I have pruned these where I could.

Roger Gellert

ACT ONE

Scene One

HALLOWES' *study, on a summer evening. It is spacious and comfortable, furnished in a clean, light, modern style, large writing desk, sofa, armchairs, bookshelves. Pictures: Dutch interiors, two competent British landscapes. No school groups, cups, or photographs. There is a reassuring air, as of old wine in new bottles.*

HALLOWES *and* PARK, *his Head of House, are in armchairs, staring into space, lost in debate.* HALLOWES *sucks at a pipe,* PARK *taps with his pencil on a piece of paper. There is an atmosphere of impasse; they have been at it for ages. When the Curtain goes up, several seconds elapse before* HALLOWES *speaks.*

HALLOWES: Difficult, isn't it?

PARK: Jolly difficult, sir.

HAMILTON: Do you think we're *ever* going to decide? (*Looks at his watch.*) Almost nine o'clock, and we don't seem any nearer. – I suppose we ought to be courageous. (*Pause.*)

PARK: Yes, sir. (*Pause.*)

HALLOWES: But it *is* Cock House match.

PARK: Yes.

HALLOWES: Read out *your* team again.

PARK (*reading*): Me, Andersen, Clayton, Tully, Bradshaw, Barnes, Gray, John Napier, Beckford, Napier minor, and Groves.

HALLOWES (*sucking at his pipe*): Yes. (*Suck, suck, suck.*) Do you think it's really the moment to launch Bradshaw?

PARK: Well, I had Beckford going flat out at him in the nets this afternoon. He's getting more confidence. He made some lovely strokes.

HALLOWES: But his fielding, Park – he's the most hopeless butter-fingers.

PARK: I must see that he has lots of practice.

HALLOWES: Yes. (*Suck, suck, suck.*) Now why drop Bennett? He did pretty well against Leighton's, you know. And didn't he get you out in the House Game last week?

PARK: That's true.

HALLOWES: But you want to drop him in favour of Bradshaw. I don't see what it is you've got against him.

PARK: He and Sands are always showing off and fooling about.

HALLOWES: You include Sands in this too, then?

PARK: Yes, sir, I do, really.

HALLOWES: Yes, I see. Don't they enjoy the game? Bennett's always seemed very keen to me.

PARK: In *his* sort of way, yes, but –

HALLOWES: Now be reasonable; we can't all enjoy things in exactly the same way –

PARK: No, sir, I know –

HALLOWES (*laughing.*): Live and let live, Park! Everyone has his own idea of what's cricket!

No response from PARK, *who looks uneasily to the ground.*

You seem rather to have it in for those two, I don't know why. (*Pause.*) Eh, Park?

PARK: Well, sir, actually, they are a bit of a problem to me, as Head of House.

HALLOWES: In what way? Do they go against discipline?

PARK: Not openly, no. It's hard to say, I – sir, as a matter of fact, I've been meaning to ask your advice about it. It's something rather outside my scope.

HALLOWES (*with a glance at his watch.*): Yes, well, you must tell me about it, Park, but I'm afraid I'll have to put you off for a few minutes. I've got Turner and Hamilton coming along any moment now for my 'set piece'.

PARK: Set piece, sir?

HALLOWES: My – well, the facts of life, and so on. You know roughly how long that takes –

PARK (*nodding reminiscently*): Oh yes, sir, I think so –

HALLOWES: Come back, say, about

half-past nine. I should be through by then.

PARK (*rising*): Right, sir. Thanks awfully. (*Moves to go.*)

HALLOWES: Have you talked it over with the other prefects or not?

PARK: Only with Tully, sir, as second Head of House. I might bring him along too, if that would be all right.

HALLOWES (*rising and going to the desk to fill his pipe*): Certainly, do. Provided he'll let us get a word in edgeways now and then!

A knock at the door.

Oh, this'll be the babes coming. (*Calls out*) Hang on a moment, will you? (*To PARK*) Look here, Park. I think we'll delay putting up the team till tomorrow, when we've got this thing about Bennett properly thrashed out. What does Tully think, by the way?

PARK: I don't think he has views on it, sir.

HALLOWES: Do you mean to say there's something he hasn't got views on? Good heavens! Well, then, let the children in, and you come back later.

PARK *again moves to go.*

It's your decision, Park, not mine, but – we'll see, shall we?

PARK: Yes, thank you, sir – about half-past nine, then, sir. (*Exit, and says outside the door*) You can go in now.

Enter TURNER *and* HAMILTON.

HALLOWES: Ah, Turner, come in. Come in, Hamilton. Sit down and make yourselves comfortable.

The boys sit. HALLOWES *leans against the desk, lighting and adjusting his pipe.*

You got a good third report from Major Bostock, Hamilton. Well done. (*Turning to* TURNER *with nervous geniality*) I wish I could say as much for you, Turner.

TURNER: Oh dear, sir.

HALLOWES: Well, you managed a remarkable off-break as I was passing the nets yesterday. You could be another Laker.

TURNER: I don't think cricket's my game, sir actually. I wish it was the rugger season.

HALLOWES: Really? Last winter you kept expressing a wish for the cricket season. What *would* please you? Shall we start some inter-House ping-pong?

TURNER (*laughing, with sarcasm*): Oh, ha ha, sir.

HALLOWES (*indulgently aping him*): Ha ha, Turner. (*He returns to his armchair.*) Well, now (*suck, suck, suck*) I dare say you both know why I've asked you to come along tonight. I – er – I expect you know that I give a talk to everyone, when they've been in the House a term or two, about the – tricky business of growing up. I could just about retire in comfort if I had a bob for every time I've given this talk, and yet I still catch myself now and then sounding a bit, well, apologetic about mentioning it at all. (*He coughs.*) You see, my generation was brought up to be a little frightened of sex. Our schoolmasters talked as if it was something slightly shameful – a necessary evil, but not awfully . . . nice. I've learned better since, of course, but that sort of thing leaves its mark.

  Now it's just what I don't want, for you to grow up feeling uneasy and ashamed about it. You're old enough now for me to be able to talk to you like sensible chaps. (*Suck, suck, suck.*)

  The first thing to get hold of . . . is that there's nothing, in itself, *bad* or *indecent* about it. – Oh, by the way, if I say anything you don't quite follow, you won't be afraid to stop me and ask, will you?

TURNER and HAMILTON: No, sir.

HALLOWES: You see – God wouldn't have given us sex if it wasn't natural and . . . and indeed a beautiful thing. There's nothing shameful about it. It's a natural function, like . . . manufacturing blood, or growing finger-nails.

  Now it may have occurred to you – it may not, I don't know – but sometimes, when you've gone to pump ship, you may have noticed that your, well, the part of you which you use for that, is beginning to develop rather more noticeably than the rest of you.

That's to say it looks as if it's . . . growing into something which . . . has a further purpose. D'you follow me?

TURNER: Yes, sir.

HALLOWES: Hamilton?

HAMILTON: Yes, thank you, sir.

HALLOWES (*affably*): Good. Now – do you think you can see what that purpose might be? Hamilton?

HAMILTON *hesitates*.

Something, I mean, less – er, commonplace?

HAMILTON (*at random*): Pleasure, sir?

HALLOWES (*collecting himself*): No – no, not pleasure exactly.

TURNER (*helpfully*): Could it be propagation-of-the-species, sir?

HALLOWES: Well, that's more like it. But of course there's much more to it than that. It would be a mistake to think of it as – how shall I put it? – just a biological device. No, it's intended for the final expression of love between a man and woman. It's the consummation of love.

TURNER: Sir –

HALLOWES: Yes, Turner.

TURNER: Sir, I'm sorry to interrupt, sir, but I wonder if I could ask something?

HALLOWES: Of course, Turner; that's all right. What is it?

TURNER: Sir, you remember Mulraine, a term or so ago?

HALLOWES (*with some unwillingness*): Yes.

TURNER: Sir – well – I thought he'd been having a – how shall I put it? – a consummation with one of the maids. And he got sacked, sir, didn't he?

HALLOWES: Yes, well – (*he clears his throat*) – that wasn't a case of love, Turner. He was simply using that girl for his pleasure, without any thought of her future. That was just a dirty mind and a dash of bravado.

TURNER (*hesitating, with tremendous seriousness*): Sir, what I don't see is – well, I don't really see how you can *tell* when it's love, sir. I mean, does it affect your . . . body differently? I mean, it would be useful to know, sir.

HALLOWES (*with a little laugh*): It would be very useful. But I'm afraid one's only got one's judgment to rely on.

HAMILTON: Sir.

HALLOWES: Yes.

HAMILTON (*in an agony of embarrassment*): Well, sir – I wonder if you could – you see, I'm afraid I don't know much about it, and I – if you could sort of – well, I mean, I don't quite see what Mulraine and the maid were doing. – I hope you don't mind my asking, sir.

TURNER *rolls up his eyes to the heavens*.

HALLOWES: Of course not, Hamilton. There's nothing wrong in honest curiosity. In fact this is something you ought to know. – Well – (*suck, suck, suck*) – you'll have noticed that men and women are . . . built differently. You can see that even with their clothes on. Now if you saw a woman without her clothes on – which I'm assuming you haven't as yet – eh, Hamilton? –

HAMILTON *blushes scarlet, while* TURNER *has subdued hysterics*.

– good – you'd see that her body was designed to fit perfectly with a man's body. You could say that she's concave where he's convex; or, if you like, she's the lock and he's the key. Well, in the act of physical love, the male and female bodies fit together in this way, and that's how they achieve the . . . consummation of love. That's how it was with Mulraine and the maid.

TURNER: But you mean, sir, that was bad because he didn't love her?

HALLOWES: That's more or less what I mean.

TURNER: Well, sir, why – why did he want to do it, then, sir?

HALLOWES: That's a very good question, Turner, and it bears on the real point of this talk, as it affects you boys here at school – (*suck, suck, suck*) – Now, the age you're getting to is when a boy starts to turn into a man. All sorts of things happen in the process: your voice breaks, and settles on to a deeper note; you'll find you have to begin to shave; and so on. And inside you, you're beginning to . . . to manufacture the . . . human seed, which you use . . . which later on you'll be able to use . . . to enable a woman to bear a child. – Well, now, as this sexual energy's beginning to make itself felt, you'll find that you look at women in a different way; you'll start to consider them as potential partners, and that's the proper instinct working in you. But of course, in a monastic institution like a school, this isn't an easy time. There aren't many women around, are there – only a few matrons and maids and housemasters' wives – not very much for you to look at?

TURNER (*gallantly*): Oh, I don't know, sir.

HALLOWES (*smiling*): Good of you to say so, Turner – No, but what naturally happens is that feelings develop between boys. An older boy often has a protective feeling for a younger one – protective like an elder brother – and sometimes this gets mixed with a more . . . romantic element. – (*He takes out a handkerchief and blows his nose.*) I do want to make it absolutely clear that there's nothing wrong with this in itself. It's likely enough that one day you may be bowled over by a pretty face in the Quad – well, goodness knows there's nothing to be ashamed of in that. What *is* wrong is for any sort of . . . physical contact to come of it. It's a temptation that you must put right behind you. You're quite clear on that?

TURNER and HAMILTON (*as one boy*): Yes, sir.

HALLOWES: There's no harm at all in an older boy wanting to help a younger one. Or a younger one admiring an older one, come to that, as long as it doesn't grow into a . . . a sloppy sort of hero-worship. But a young boy isn't a girl, and it's not very manly for him to be treated like one; and it can have a very damaging effect on him. So if this should ever concern either of you, you must value very strongly the friendship and unselfishness in it, and utterly turn your back on anything which could

spoil it or . . . turn it into unworthiness. – At its best, the experience can be very uplifting.

TURNER (*speaking with an air of ill-disguised pastiche*); Sir, would you say that it could give you a glimpse of the sort of love you'll give to a woman some day, sir, and, I mean, you'll try to keep yourself clean in – er – body and soul, as you'd want her to be, sir?

HALLOWES (*surprised*): Yes, I would. (*Pause*) Turner, you haven't attended one of these functions before, have you, by any chance?

TURNER: Yes, sir, last term. I came with Buller.

HALLOWES: Good gracious. (*He refers to his papers.*) You weren't crossed off. Well, I think it might have been a good idea to have mentioned that before, don't you?

TURNER: Well, sir, I thought perhaps you wanted to see how much I'd remembered. Sort of revision test, sir.

The telephone on HALLOWES' *desk rings.*

HALLOWES: Bother! I'm sorry. (*He goes and answers the 'phone.*) Hello. Yes. Oh, hello, Hemming. – Yes. Oh, good lord, yes, I am sorry, I completely forgot. Yes, it may be here. – (*He searches among the books on his desk.*) Just a moment – no, it doesn't seem to be. Probably in the other room somewhere. Look, I won't keep you hanging on. I'll find the thing and ring you back in a couple of minutes. Will that be all right, Hemming? – No, no trouble. Goodbye for the moment. (*He puts the 'phone down.*) I must just see to this. Will you sit tight for a minute or two?

TURNER and HAMILTON: Yes, sir.

HALLOWES: I suppose I haven't got the book in here – (*he peers at a certain shelf*) – no, I thought not. – Well, hang on, then.

TURNER and HAMILTON: Righto, sir.

Exit HALLOWES. *When he is well out of earshot,* TURNER *speaks.*

TURNER: Well, Crab – feeling sexy?

HAMILTON: No, why?

TURNER: I thought all this might have touched some sleeping chord in you. About time *something* did.

HAMILTON: It's not very exciting.

TURNER: That's what you think. (*He gets up and stretches.*) Honestly, Crab, you are the most helpless vestal virgin. I bet your grandfather was a whitebait or something. I feel jolly sorry for you sometimes. You're so dull!

HAMILTON: Thanks.

TURNER: Don't you love that bit about being 'bowled over by a pretty face in the Quad'! I'm mad about that. Gosh, I'd like to see you bowl someone over, you old drip.

HAMILTON: I don't think *I* would.

TURNER: Well, you won't at the rate you're going, so that's all right.

HAMILTON: Look – do you mind if I ask you something?

TURNER: Go on – what?

HAMILTON: Well – everyone knows I'm – not very well up in – sex and stuff –

TURNER: Oh, ask Uncle Turner. And – (*imitating* HALLOWES) – if I say anything you don't understand, don't hesitate to stop me and buy one.

HAMILTON: Well – I know you – see a lot of the seniors – but what do you *do* with them all the time? I hope you don't mind me asking.

TURNER: Crikey, you're incredible! I just get into bed with them, and things like that.

HAMILTON: But – whatever for?

TURNER: Pleasure, Crab. You were right first time. Not propagaggers, thank God.

HAMILTON: But you're not – concave, are you?

TURNER: Oh, blimey. You don't *have* to go turning keys in locks, you know.

HAMILTON: But – however did you start, in the first place?

TURNER: Oh, lord, years ago! I came down to the drying-room one night to fetch a towel, and one of the pre's was there, and he said, 'Come back in an hour's time,' so I did. Do you want the details?

(*He leans against* HALLOWES' *desk.*)

HAMILTON: No, no – it's all right, thanks. But why is it so secret?

TURNER: Well, you don't suppose it's allowed, do you? It's not only beaks that have a thing about it; there's parents. If they get a sniff, you've had it. Outraged letters, heaven knows what; you've no idea. Don't you remember the fuss about Walford last term?

HAMILTON: I don't understand it.

TURNER: Oh, you poor thing.

HAMILTON (*stuffily*): It isn't very manly.

TURNER: Oh, dry up. There's nothing cissy about it. Anyway, do you call yourself a fine example of manliness?

HAMILTON: I suppose not.

TURNER: Well, there you are – Crab, isn't it a bit boring, putting on your pyjamas, and brushing your teeth, and getting into bed, night after night, without a hope of anything happening?

HAMILTON: Something did happen once, as a matter of fact. Someone came along in the dark and tried to get into my bed, so I gave him a push and he went away. Anyway I thought he was sleep-walking or something. Do you think he wanted to come in with me?

TURNER: I don't know. I expect so. Who was it?

HAMILTON: Webster, I think.

TURNER: Oh, bad luck. Look, suppose someone like Bennett asked you – what would you do?

HAMILTON: Honestly, I wouldn't –

TURNER (*diving back to his chair and adopting a demure attitude*): Psst! Here's the Old Man coming. For God's sake look moral. As if you could help it.

Enter HALLOWES, *with an open book.*

HALLOWES: Awfully sorry, you two. (*Goes to the 'phone and picks it up.*) Mr. Hemming, please. – Hemming? Hallowes here. Sorry to keep you waiting; the wretched thing had hidden itself in the most unsuitable place. – Yes, I've found the title you want. Got a pencil? – Yes. *Succession in Thessaly*, by L.C. Bissett. – L.C. Bissett. Right? – Don't mention it. Good night, Hemming. (*He rings off, heaving a sigh.*) Well, now – (*suck, suck, suck*) – I was saying – (*suck, suck*) – that these friendships could be valuable, and I've nothing against them myself. But they do –

A knock at the door. HALLOWES *looks at his watch.*

Half-past nine.

(*He calls out:*) Come in! (PARK *puts his head round the door.*)

Park, would you mind just holding on a minute – I haven't quite finished yet.

PARK: No, sir, right. (*He retires.*)

HALLOWES: Did you think of any questions you wanted clearing up while I was out of the room?

TURNER'*s face controls itself with difficulty.*

HAMILTON: No, thank you, sir.

HALLOWES: Turner?

TURNER: No, sir, I don't think so.

HALLOWES: Well, you're both sensible fellows and you won't let me down.

HAMILTON: Oh, no, sir.

TURNER: Of course not, sir.

HALLOWES: Good. Then we'll call it a day, shall we? – Now, any time you're faced with a problem, I want you to feel you can come straight in here and talk it over. You know I want to help you in any way I can, and I'm never too busy to have a chat.

TURNER: Thank you, sir.

HALLOWES: Right you are, then. Up to bed, and don't make too much noise.

TURNER and HAMILTON: No, sir. Goodnight, sir.

HALLOWES: Goodnight, both of you. Let the others come in.

HAMILTON *moves to the door, opens it and goes out, but* TURNER *following, stands aside to let* PARK *come in.* TULLY *comes after* PARK, *and* TURNER, *as he draws abreast, gives an infinitesimal leer, to which* TULLY *responds with a threatening motion, also infinitesimal. Exit* TURNER.

PARK: I brought Tully along, sir.

HALLOWES (*indicating chairs*): Good. Sit down, do. Well, now, Park. Let's hear what the situation is.

TULLY (*getting in first*): Sir, I ought to say that I'm here rather under protest, really. I want to support Mike, but I do think he's got this out of proportion.

HALLOWES (*holding up a hand*): Just a moment, Tully! Give him a chance to speak!

PARK: Well, sir, I – it's a matter of House discipline, really, but I think I ought to put it into your hands. The thing is that certain boys – I haven't got any cast-iron evidence, of course, it's rather impossible to, but – I'm pretty sure there's some . . . filthy behaviour going on, and I feel it's up to me to stop it.

HALLOWES: You mean . . . sexual trouble?

PARK (*swallowing hard*): Yes, sir. To be quite honest, it isn't a thing I really feel competent to deal with on my own. I don't understand it enough. I don't know how to set about it. – And John doesn't agree with me, anyway–

TULLY: No, sir.

PARK: – and I haven't talked it over with anyone else yet.

HALLOWES: I see. Well, you were right to come and discuss it. It's a tricky business, and there's no one way of going about it. – Now this is between us and these four walls, and I think you'd better give me an idea who's involved and how seriously.

TULLY: Sir, sorry to barge in, but do you think it's, I mean, quite fair to start giving names until you've heard Mike's account of it and decided whether you think it *is* serious? Because I'm certain it's mostly wind.

HALLOWES: That's a fair point, Tully. But I think I can honestly say that knowing their names won't prejudice me, and it will be easier to weigh the thing up.

PARK: That's what I thought, sir. – Well, the one I'm most doubtful about – sir, what is your opinion of Sands?

HALLOWES: Sands. Oh, he's not so black as he paints himself. He's going through his Shelley period and pretending to be an atheist – a bit like you, in fact, Tully.

TULLY *grins.*

But it's only because he enjoys arguing with me and doesn't much enjoy getting up for Early Service. He's the sort of boy I'd expect to form an attachment at his age – and it'd probably do him the world of good.

PARK: Well, yes, sir, but I don't know if you'd call this an attachment. You see, sir, there seem to be rather a lot of attachments, and whatever they're doing to him, I don't think they're doing the younger boys much good.

HALLOWES: Ah, well, then, that's another matter. Which younger boys are you thinking of?

PARK: Cowley, sir. Turner.

HALLOWES: Turner.

PARK: Yes, sir. Lomas. Wright. Kennedy.

HALLOWES (*hastily*): That'll do to be going on with. Now how do you know about these cases?

TULLY: Well, sir – sorry again, but – I think that's just it. Mike doesn't know. He's convinced himself that there's a wave of vice. But, sir, you know the sort of Lower School stuff. They're so dirty-minded at that age – it doesn't mean a thing, but they talk the most monstrous tripe if they want to impress somebody. I think there might be a case for trying to clean up conversation a bit, but honestly, sir, I think we'd do far more harm than good if we went and launched a vice campaign – anti-vice, I mean. Mike's so gullible.

PARK (*unamused*): Well, with your sort of attitude –

HALLOWES (*intervening*): Look, hold on a second. I see both points of view, and if anything, Tully, I'm inclined to agree with yours. But what you must remember is that I'm here *in loco parentis* – I'm deputising for the parents of these children, and I have to make it my business to see that they aren't exposed to any undesirable influences. That's my responsibility. And Park's responsibility as Head of House is to keep me thoroughly informed of what goes on.

PARK: Well, sir, I do what I can.

HALLOWES: You do very well. I've got complete confidence in you, and don't mind what Tully says.

PARK: Oh, I don't, sir. He's a cross I have to bear. Very good for me, I suppose.

TULLY: You know you love bearing crosses.

HALLOWES: Can we get back to our muttons? Apart from Sands, who do you think are mixed up in this business?

PARK: I'm not sure about Bennett, sir. I thought he overdid the love-interest in the House play rather much.

TULLY (*despairingly*): I ask you.

PARK: Cowley, you remember, sir.

HALLOWES: A very pretty flapper Cowley made.

TULLY: It's such a seedy old dig at the drama, sir. Park's the sort of Roundhead who's ready to close anything down just in case it's immoral. – Come on, sir, support me. I shan't be allowed to produce *Richard III* at this rate.

HALLOWES (*smiling*): I do support you, Tully. Though fortunately *Richard III* is the Headmaster's pigeon, not mine.

TULLY: I'm only afraid Mike may shoot down so many good things in the process. It's like – oh, I don't know – deciding that woods are nicer with bluebells, so you cut down all the trees to give the soil more light. No, that's not it, but you know what I mean.

HALLOWES: I know what you mean. – Well, Park, who else?

PARK: Langford, sir. I found a poem of his lying about. Pretty suggestive, I thought.

HALLOWES: For example?

PARK (*embarrassed*): Oh – well – as far as I remember –

TULLY: Go on.

PARK: Something about kissing a boy's hair.

TULLY: Absolute proof of innocence. Do you think he'd be bothering to *write* about it if he were *doing* it?

HALLOWES *laughs.*

PARK: Then there's Leeming, too.

TULLY: The pale young curate! You see, sir, it's absurd.

PARK: Oh, do shut up.

TULLY: Pale with nameless desires, of course.

HALLOWES (*with firmness*): Be quiet, Tully. I want to hear what Park's got to say, if you don't mind. – Still, Park – (*little laugh*) – I don't think we need go so far as to suspect Leeming of subversion. Tell me what you know about Sands.

TULLY: Sir, Sands isn't known to have done anything worse than have Lomas in for tea and Keats.

HALLOWES: I must say I can't help feeling optimistic while this general air of Eisteddfod persists. Are there any *un*poetic boys involved in it, Park?

TULLY *makes to interpose.*

If Tully will give you a chance to speak.

PARK: Bennett's jolly unpoetic, sir. And honestly I don't trust Sands much either. You see, the remarks I've heard from some of the Lower School – they're not very nice, sir. I heard Turner saying some disgusting things.

HALLOWES: And you're sure it was autobiography?

TULLY: Fiction, sir. Science fiction. Stream of thought. I don't pretend Turner's mind is as the driven snow.

HALLOWES: He's a very amusing little boy; very polite. Perhaps too polite. One can't tell what goes on behind that. – Well, now, look here. It does seem to me that this is something we've got to watch very carefully. And I know you will, Park. On the other hand, as I take it you haven't actually found anyone – *in flagrante delicto* – you follow me?

TULLY: Yes, sir. But if Mike had his way –

HALLOWES (*breaking in*): Quiet, Tully. You're rather trying at times, you

know. – Now, Park, I don't think there's any action you can take at the moment. But I want you prefects to keep your eyes skinned from now on. There's no sense in putting our heads in the sand and pretending these things don't exist, because they do. – The important thing is that you should consult me before you take any measures. It's always a delicate matter, and I'm very much against indiscriminately sitting on all friendships between boys of different ages – provided it *is* friendship. – There's such a thing as Christian love. Our job is to see that it doesn't lapse into the profane.

PARK: Yes, sir, quite.

HALLOWES: Better keep a special eye on Turner. I might have a talk with him myself. – No, I won't do that yet. But if you catch him in any of this dirty talk again, make him understand that he may be taken seriously. See how he reacts. A bit of a scare wouldn't do that lad any harm. – Anyway, for the moment I'm going to leave it in your hands, Park. Get the truth if you can.

PARK: I will, sir.

He and TULLY *rise.*

HALLOWES: We can't delay the House Team any longer, though. You must do as you think best. Play Bradshaw, and let's keep our fingers crossed.

PARK: Right, sir, thank you.

HALLOWES: But, Park, this other matter – no disciplinary action, mind you. Just the truth.

PARK: I'll get it, sir.

Quick curtain

Scene Two

The curtain rises on TULLY's *study, empty.*

It is a tiny room, like a prison cell, and the walls are coated with shiny, toffee-coloured paint. A remarkable quantity of cheap, seedy and battered furniture is somehow crammed into the little space. Two dying armchairs, two hard chairs, a

*motley bookshelf, a small provisions
cupboard, a tuck-box, cricket bat and
pads, an electric fire in front of the walled
up fireplace, books piled high on the
mantelpiece. Hung on the wall above the
mantelpiece, a guitar. Also on the walls
the following pictures:* The Wavy
Cornfield *and* Portrait of a Young Man *by
Van Gogh;* David's portrait of Napoleon;
*framed photographs of Generals
Alexander and Rommel; Rouault's* La
Mariée; *a pouncing horse by Delacroix;
and other pictures by Goya, Gauguin and
Toulouse-Lautrec. In the window, a
statuette of Garibaldi.*

*It is next morning, and time for the break
between lessons. Outside, a confused
noise of whistling, walking and running
in stone-paved corridors.*

*The door bursts angrily open and
TULLY comes in, followed by PARK.
Both are carrying books.*

TULLY: Oh, come on, say it, for God's
sake. I let you down. Come on; I can't
stand mute reproach any longer. You
knew I didn't agree with you. Why the
heck did you ask me to come?

PARK: I thought you'd help to thrash it
out, not spend all the time trying to
make me look a B.F.

TULLY: That's tripe. You needed the
support; you always do. Why start a
witch-hunt? It'll leave you a nervous
wreck, however it leaves the House.
Let it be.

PARK: You don't approve of this filth, do
you?

TULLY (*with burning insincerity*): Good
God, Mungo, you know me. What do
you mean?

PARK: Well, you seem to do nothing but
obstruct. You say it's always with us;
well, it shouldn't be. And it wouldn't, if
Heads of House weren't so gutless or
lazy as a rule.

TULLY: Or involved themselves.

PARK: Or that, I suppose, yes. Well, the
least I can do is have a stab at it. I
shouldn't think much of myself if I just
accepted it.

TULLY: I should think much more of
you.

PARK: But why?

TULLY: Because it's *natural*, that's why.
We can't outlaw it just because you
and I don't happen to be affected. For
heaven's sake, didn't you ever have a
sex talk from the Old Man?

PARK: I went with you.

TULLY: Happy days. Well, you know
what he says; no women, and the
instinct's got to settle for something.

PARK: All right, let them have tender
feelings if they must, but I'm not having
little beasts like Turner tarting around.

TULLY: But you can't stop it – even if
it's true, which I doubt. And as for
your getting the truth out of Turner,
honestly, Mungo, can you see yourself
doing it? (*He roars with laughter.*) I
can. You'd either reduce the boy to
hysterics, or scare him out of his wits.
Honestly, old thing, you'll make
yourself look an absolute ass. You'll
be so bad at it. Even I could do better.

PARK: You probably could. – Look, why
don't you?

TULLY: *Me?*

PARK: Yes.

TULLY: Him being my fag, you mean?

PARK: Not so much that, but you know
they're rather used to me being stodgy
about things –

TULLY *makes a deprecating noise.*

they rather expect it. But you're
considered, well, a bit of a dog –

TULLY: Woof!

PARK: They'd listen to you. John, I'd be
terribly grateful . . . (*Pause.*)

TULLY: I dunno.

PARK: You're so much more popular
than me –

TULLY (*without conviction*): What utter
tripe!

PARK: Yes, it's true. I was quite popular
before I was Head of House, but not
now. – I'm sorry, don't let's talk about
that. Will you do it for me?

TULLY: All right, Mungo. If you really
want me to. I suppose we're both
concerned with the truth, even if we
can't agree what to do with it.

PARK: Yes, the truth matters more than a

few silly little boys. It's the House I'm thinking of.

TULLY: Oh, heavens, I'm not doing it for the House. Just for my dear old chum. (*He punches* PARK *lightly in the midriff.*)

PARK (*moved*): Come off it.

TULLY: Leave it to Uncle.

PARK: How will you work round to it?

TULLY: Turner? Ask for his views on Kinsey.

PARK (*horrified*): Ask for his – Good Lord, you had me worried for a moment.

TULLY: Ask him how many times a week – no, don't worry, though, I'll think of something.

PARK (*suddenly apprehensive*): John, you won't muck it up, will you? You must take it seriously.

TULLY: Look, if I don't get the truth from him, I give you full permission to move in with thumbscrews.

PARK: I know you think I've got a bee in my bonnet about this. Well, all right, I have. But honestly, I know what I'm talking about. I made up my mind some time ago to stamp the whole dirty thing out.

TULLY: You made up your mind – when?

PARK: Oh . . . when I became Head of House.

TULLY: Any particular reason?

PARK: No. Well . . . yes, if you want to know, there was. As a matter of fact – (*Pause.*)

TULLY: As a matter of fact –?

PARK: Well, something happened to me once which shook me. Not so very long ago, come to that.

Pause. PARK *is in an agony of embarrassment about the confession he is going to make. He is sitting in one of the armchairs, rolling and unrolling the rubber grip on the handle of* TULLY's *cricket bat.* TULLY *is sitting on an arm of the other armchair, slightly behind and above him.*

You remember Hardyman?

TULLY: Yes, I remember him. Something funny about his leaving, wasn't there?

PARK: That's right. Well, I'll tell you what happened about him.

TULLY: Please.

PARK: You'll keep it to yourself.

TULLY: Let me die else.

PARK (*it would be tedious to indicate all the hesitations in his story*): It was about a year ago. That night we had the great battle with Clifford's, do you remember?

TULLY: After they beat us in Cock House match.

PARK: That's right. There were lots of us fighting through their top dormitory. You were probably there yourself.

TULLY: No, I was fighting on another front.

PARK: Well, anyway, I ran into Hardyman, and we had a terrific scrap. Nothing serious, you know, just for the fun of the thing. I rather liked him, actually. Then.

TULLY: He seemed pleasant enough.

PARK: Seemed, yes. Well, at one point things had rather fizzled out, and he said he was tired of all this fooling, and what about a drink. So we went along to his study, and he'd got a brand new bottle of whisky. I'd hardly ever had whisky, actually, and I hated it, but I didn't like to say so, and I drank quite a lot, and we talked about cricket and things – at least, I did, but he was always dragging the conversation round to sex. But I'd got over hating the whisky by this time, and I'd had a good bit, and I just laughed. I don't know why, but I laughed and laughed, as if it was all damned funny, but it wasn't, it was foul. (*He stops abruptly.*)

TULLY: Go on.

PARK: Well – (*Pause.*) Well, after a bit we started fighting again, not that there was much room in that study, but we did, anyway. And then, I can't remember how it happened, but we got pretty well jammed right under his desk, and I couldn't move because he was on top of me – he was quite a big chap, you know. And he started to sort of bite me, all over my neck, and I was still laughing and trying to get him off, but I couldn't, and then he was licking my face, just like a dog, and I tried to stop him – I was pretty tight, I suppose, but I didn't like that – and then I suddenly realised he was trying to – well, I knew it wasn't a game anymore – not my kind, anyway. And do you know what he said?

TULLY: What did he say?

PARK: God, he was – I don't know – I can't remember just what he said –

TULLY: Nonsense, of course you can.

PARK: I can't, John, honestly, I – I don't remember now. But he was saying these bloody awful things, and fumbling about. – Then I just went mad. I got him off somehow, and I hit him three or four times so hard that I knocked him out, and I just went on hitting his face after that, and finally he looked such a mess I felt sick, and I ran back here, and went straight in to the Old Man and told him everything. He must have thought I was barmy. – But anyway, Hardyman didn't come back next term.

TULLY (*genuinely impressed*): Hm.

PARK: It's so filthy, that sort of thing. I don't know if it ever happened to you. But it's foul.

TULLY: Poor old chap. I see your point.

PARK: It's just that I see red when I think of little worms like Turner messing around like that.

TULLY: Of course you do. Trouble is, though, that in ways you really are like those Inquisition boys. I mean, you're a Christian – oughtn't you to be saving people by love, not hate?

PARK: Oh, that's not fair, now –

TULLY: I think it is, though, Mungo. Look, if you genuinely want to save Turner's soul, why be so concerned what happens to his body? The mind's a muckheap anyhow, and you're not going to change that.

PARK: I can try.

TULLY: You want to impose your own likes and dislikes on other people – that's all you're doing.

PARK: You should talk! You and your fascism and atheism –

TULLY: I am *not* a fascist! *You* are a fascist.

PARK: Well, you're an atheist.

TULLY: All right, so I'm an atheist. But it's not because I (*aping* HALLOWES) 'don't like getting up for Early Service'. I should adore to get up for Early Service. The trouble is, I don't happen to believe in it, that's all. I've got to be honest. It's nothing to do with likes and dislikes. I'm trying to act on principle.

PARK: Well, so am I.

TULLY: Then go easy with the jackboots. You're a practising Christian, you've got to love everybody however much you hate them – isn't that true? Whereas all I've got to do is keep my self-respect.

PARK: It must make life pretty easy.

TULLY: Simple, anyway. Come on, though, admit that I'm indispensable.

PARK (*smiling*): At the moment, yes. Shall I send Turner?

TULLY: No, it's OK. I'll yell for him.

PARK: Then I'm clearing out. Thanks a hell of a lot. If you'll just do this for me, I can handle the rest.

TULLY (*aping* HALLOWES *again*): I have every confidence in you. – Well, here goes. (*He opens the door and bellows into the corridor.*) Boy!!

PARK: I'd better make myself scarce. Good luck, John.

TULLY: C'est un morceau de gâteau.

Exit PARK. *Running feet approach and stop outside.*

Turner! A word with you.

Enter TURNER.

TURNER: Hullo, master.

The door is shut, and the scene which follows is one of complete intimacy.

TULLY (*shaking his head*): I wish I could fit you with a silencer.

TURNER: Why, am I fired?

TULLY: Not yet, I hope. – Now listen, rabbit. Uncle Park suspects you of grave sexual misdemeanour. He has charged me to give you the dressing-down of your life.

TURNER: Oh.

TULLY: We are all very angry with you in the common-room. We shall probably expel you.

TURNER: How awful. The disgrace.

TULLY: The disgrace.

TURNER: You too?

TULLY: You see I am still at large.

TURNER: You dirty old hypocrite! I suppose Park really thinks you're ferreting out my guilty secrets. I passed him in the passage, looking significant.

TULLY: You're jolly lucky he didn't undertake you himself. He'd have demolished you.

TURNER: Go on! He's rather nice. I'd have changed his mind.

TULLY: You think so? I'm afraid you'd have been killed in action. Park is very highly combustible these days. You make the great mistake of thinking that everyone's as randy as you, if they'd only admit it. You believe that anyone can be seduced under favourable circumstances. But you're wrong. If there is any bit of Park that could desire you, it's too many fathoms deep to be worth fishing for.

TURNER *makes to interrupt.*

No, seriously, though – he's on the war-path. You must keep that mouth of yours shut a bit more.

TURNER: I'm sorry, John.

TULLY: Well, it's all right this time, because I'm pulling the most monstrous confidence trick on him. I shall give you a certificate of blameless behaviour, and say that your careless talk was pure fantasy, and the old silly will take it like a lamb.

TURNER: Good. (*Pause.*) And, incidentally –

TULLY: Mm?

TURNER: You know you said there were some people you can't . . . seduce?

TULLY: Yes.

TURNER: Well, I want to see if that's true.

TULLY: Oh, no, look, if you're going to make a pass at old Park just for the hell of it, we may as well pack our bags.

TURNER: I wasn't thinking of Park, actually; I wasn't even thinking of myself.

TULLY: Astonishing. Who – had you in mind?

TURNER (*after a due pause*): Have you ever considered Hamilton?

TULLY: Not often, I must say. What as?

TURNER: Well, I wish you would, just for a lark! I give you full permission. It interests me.

TULLY: Hamilton! Oh, *no*.

TURNER: He's quite nice looking. You said so yourself once.

TULLY: Yes, but in such a wet sort of way. The shock would kill him, I should think.

TURNER: Oh, go on! It might do him a bit of good.

TULLY: You might think of me for a moment. I'm not a sort of emotional stud bull.

TURNER: Oh, do!

TULLY: What a monster you are, really. No, thanks. I am not inspired by Hamilton's virginity. Sorry.

TURNER: We'll see.

TULLY: We shall. (*Pause.*) Though as a matter of fact –

TURNER (*alert*): Mm?

TULLY: It wouldn't be altogether without interest.

TURNER: Ha! Now you're talking.

TULLY: The average boy, as you know, is only too horribly willing. – Hamilton would be a real problem. Rather fascinating. I wonder –

TURNER: You mustn't cheat.

TULLY: Good lord, no. It would be a pure exercise in strategy.

TURNER: I wonder what Rommel would have done . . .

TULLY: I see Hamilton as a sort of minor Jericho; the only way to get through would be by cracking him at the foundations. I think I see how, too. A period of uncertainty and sniping first, with a bit of scattered artillery fire. The walls tremble, but stand firm. Then I launch two concentrated dive-bomber attacks, on the citadel and the arsenal –

TURNER: Up the Spurs!

TULLY: And that completely disrupts communications; after which I march smartly three times round the town, blow the horns like billy-oh, and the walls come tumbling down. At least, that's the theory of the thing.

TURNER: I don't remember all this campaigning with me.

TULLY: I don't remember the need for it, as there wasn't even a show of resistance, and the defending force came trotting out with open pyjamas –

TURNER: All right, all right. Well, how will you get things moving?

TULLY: How, yes . . .

TURNER: Help him with his Latin.

TULLY: Can't see him needing that.

TURNER: Dope him.

TULLY: I admire your methods. I thought this was to be a decent seduction.

TURNER: Break his arm, and then be sympathetic.

TULLY: Charming.

TURNER: Well, get him into *Richard III*.

TULLY: Hamilton, in my play! Not likely.

TURNER: Why not? He'd be a smash hit in a wimple. It's the obvious thing.

TULLY: But what on earth could he do? He's so dreary. Too feeble to carry halberds and too wet for Princes in the Tower.

TURNER: There'll be something, you'll see. When are the auditions?

TULLY: If you ever looked at notice-boards, you'd know. I put up a long essay about it yesterday. Applications to be in by Friday.

TURNER: Well, I want to play a Little Prince and be murdered by you.

TULLY: Not in person, I'm afraid. There are hired assassins. – Besides, it's very impertinent of you to assume that I shall be playing the lead. We haven't had the auditions yet.

TURNER: Oh, come off that. Why else produce the thing? (*Pause.*)

TULLY: I suppose I can always give him a try. But he won't come of his own accord, and I can hardly ask him.

TURNER: He'll come.

TULLY: He's the last person to think of trying.

TURNER (*with conviction*): He'll come.

Pause. TULLY *begins to laugh, and* TURNER *joins him, as . . .*

The curtain falls.

ACT TWO

TULLY's study, that afternoon.

TULLY, grimacing horribly, is engaged in furious moral argument with PARK, who leans against the table.

TULLY (*ranting*): Down with education, down with the arts and sciences, down with religion and Western civilisation, down with the spirit of man! Expensive luxuries, gentlemen, and a threat to morality! (*Lifting a bottle of embrocation as for a toast.*) Gentlemen, I give you – morality! And I shan't be wanting it back!

He pretends to swig off the embrocation.

PARK: Stop being hysterical.

TULLY: Hysterical! You try to ruin my life's work, and you have the impertinence to call me hysterical, you damned muscle-bound Methodist!

PARK: I'm not ruining anything. I'm just saying: Mind how you go.

TULLY: Look, the Turner scare was nothing but wind: I don't know what you're moaning about. And how the hell can I put the bloody play on with you standing around like the kiss of death? I refuse to accept you as a watch committee. Have I got to cast all the women from members of the XV?

PARK: I didn't say that.

TULLY: Serve 'em right if I did, too. – However, the fact is that there are only two decent unbroken voices within miles and you object to both. Stop chuntering and say why.

PARK: I told you.

TULLY: You told me about Cowley. Your considered opinion was that he enjoyed being looked at too much. – Blimey! – And what's the objection to Trickett?

PARK: Too many people enjoy looking at him.

TULLY (*incredulously*): Say that again.

PARK: You heard.

Pause.

TULLY (*between laughter and blind rage*): It's beyond belief. So I must have a Queen Margaret who's terrified to go on the stage, and who everyone will loathe looking at. – Rather effective, of course, in a way. – No! No! Get out before I do you an injury! I shall have who I like in my play, and if you want to stop Cowley you'll have to break his neck.

PARK: It'll be a pleasure.

TULLY: And Trickett, unhappily, isn't under your jurisdiction. Thank God I'm not casting a House play.

PARK: But I'm serious about Cowley. What I feel is –

A knock at the door.

TULLY: Come in!

The door opens. HAMILTON is standing there, diffident and very well-washed.

Hullo.

HAMILTON: Oh, I'm sorry, Tully, I – shall I come back later?

TULLY: What was it you wanted?

HAMILTON (*crimson*): Well, I wondered if I could have an audition for *Richard III*. (*Pause.*)

PARK: John, I'm in the way. I'll be going. (*He laughs.*) This may be the very boy you need.

TULLY: Who can tell? I'll let you know.

Exit PARK.

Well – you'd better sit down.

HAMILTON *sits.*

Have you read the play?

HAMILTON: Not the whole of it, I'm afraid.

TULLY: I see. – You haven't done much acting before, have you?

HAMILTON: No, none. We're reading *King Lear* in form with Major Bostock.

TULLY: Like it?

HAMILTON: Well, it's very – impressive.

TULLY: Who reads Lear?

HAMILTON: The part of Lear?

TULLY: Yes.

HAMILTON: Major Bostock.

TULLY: I can see it would be impressive. And what do *you* read?

HAMILTON: Oh, different things. Usually Cordelia.

TULLY: Naturally.

HAMILTON *laughs uneasily.*

I should be tempted to cast you against type. Something sexy. Regan, say. – Well, the play we're going to be concerned with isn't quite up to *Lear*, I'm afraid.

HAMILTON: Oh, that's all right.

TULLY: Very good of you. Now then, what part had you in mind?

HAMILTON: Well, Turner said –

TULLY (*quickly*): Turner said?

HAMILTON (*confused*): Well, yes, we were talking about it. I think he wants to try, too.

TULLY: I see. So what did he say?

HAMILTON: He said I might try Queen Anne.

HAMILTON *sits like a well-meaning fly caught in the centre of* TULLY's *web.* TULLY *himself, a large, prickly and often cruel spider, will seldom sit during this scene, but will range round the small room, watching his victim intently, and gauging the effect of his words on him.*

TULLY: What was that?

HAMILTON: Queen Anne. (*Pause.*)

HAMILTON: Did you mean Queen Margaret, or the Lady Anne?

HAMILTON: I think I must have meant Lady Anne. Which is which?

TULLY: Queen Margaret is a vampire, a fish-wife, a brawling royal hag.

HAMILTON *gives way to mirth, then freezes again.*

Do you fancy yourself as Queen Margaret?

HAMILTON: I don't think I'd be very good.

TULLY: I hope you're not being modest, but I'll take your word for it. Perhaps I should play safe with Queen Margaret. – That leaves us with the Lady Anne. She is a very moral girl, but gets seduced. The wretched Richard has vilely slain her old man, and she resents it. She's quite as rude as Queen Meg to begin with, but she can't keep it up, and the hunchback hunches himself into bed with her. Off-stage, of course. – A difficult part, if not a big one. Now I wonder if you could attempt it. You have a moral face, but could you be seduced? (*Pause.* TULLY *is at the window, thoughtfully gazing out.*)

HAMILTON (*doubtfully*): Well, I –

TULLY (*wheeling round*): Eh?

HAMILTON: I think I'd find that a bit hard.

TULLY (*rubbing his hands*): Oh, yes. I should think it would be hard work all round. But who's afraid of work? Not you, I'm sure. I've heard you called a swot.

HAMILTON: Yes.

TULLY: A fair charge, would you say?

TULLY (*unwillingly*): I do work hard.

TULLY: Why?

HAMILTON: I don't know. I don't mind it.

TULLY: You don't mind it. There's a wonderful luke-warmness about you, isn't there? Well, I must say you don't seem to have the glassy eye of the natural scholar. Perhaps you work so as to get an advantage over the others.

HAMILTON: Oh, no, I don't think so.

TULLY: Pity. I was going to admire your dourness. Well, well. So you swot because you've found nothing better to do – as yet.

HAMILTON: Yes.

TULLY: Swots have a sort of sour, inky smell and yellow skin like something that's been left in a cupboard. And sickly hair. (*He examines* HAMILTON.) I don't notice this in you yet; but probably you're just on the turn. Another week or two and you'll have gone sour. – Well, it's no concern of mine. Let's have a look at the play.

HAMILTON: I'm afraid you don't think much of me.

TULLY: Oh, come, now.

HAMILTON: I'm wasting your time. I'd

be no good.

He rises to go.

TULLY: Sit down.

HAMILTON *sits.*

Hamilton, you're very young. You really are awfully young. How do you know what you can't do? You ought to try everything once. At least once. No harm done if you fail.

HAMILTON: Well, all right. But honestly, you mustn't expect anything. I'll be terrible.

TULLY: I expect nothing. But I don't know why you seem so determined to prejudice me against you.

HAMILTON: Oh, Tully, I'm not.

TULLY: Then let's stick to the business in hand, shall we? And have a little less whimpering. Good. Now, what'll we try first? How about a little Prince?

HAMILTON (*unenthusiastically*): All right. (*He takes out his spectacles and puts them on.*)

TULLY (*in disgust*): Do you always wear those?

HAMILTON (*apologetically*): I've got astigmatism.

TULLY: Good God.

Briskly, he takes an enormous Complete Shakespeare *and tosses it into* HAMILTON's *lap.*

Richard III is quite near the beginning.

Himself, he takes a tiny pocket edition of the play, which will not impair his manoeuvrability.

Found it?

HAMILTON: Yes, thanks.

TULLY (*flipping the pages*): Right, er, let's see, where are they, now, Act 3, I should think, somewhere – Hastings, Buckingham – no, Gloster, Duchess of York, York, that's more like it. Look, Act II, Scene 4, the beginning. 'Last night, I hear, they lay at Northampton' – got that?

HAMILTON (*after some riffling*): Yes.

TULLY: The Archbishop's saying where the Prince of Wales has got to on his way south to London, and the Duchess of York says she hopes he is much grown since last she saw him. Now, we'll read from there. You do York, and I'll do the other bits. Ready?

HAMILTON: Yes.

TULLY: 'But I hear, no; they say my son of York
Has almost overta'en him in his growth.'

HAMILTON (*reading with smooth dullness*): 'Ay, mother; but I would not have it so.'

TULLY: 'Why, my young cousin, it is good to grow.'

HAMILTON: 'Grandam, one night, as we did sit at supper,
My uncle Rivers talk'd how I did grow
More than my brother: "Ay," quoth my uncle apace –'

TULLY (*interrupting*): 'My uncle Gloster', not 'apace'; that goes on the end of the next line. (*Looks over* HAMILTON's *shoulder.*) I must say it is rather confusingly printed. Back to '"Ay," quoth my uncle . . .'

HAMILTON: '. . . "Ay," quoth my uncle Gloster,
"Small herbs have grace, great weeds do grow apace":
And since, methinks, I would not grow so fast,
Because sweet flowers are slow, and weeds make haste.'

TULLY: Competent sight-reading, not much sense and no interest. I quite see how you gain your academic successes, but it won't do for the stage. Look at it again.

HAMILTON *studies;* TULLY *paces about.*

You made complete nonsense of the last couplet, of course. 'Since' doesn't mean 'because', you know; it means 'since then', 'since that day', do you see?

HAMILTON: Oh, I see, yes. I hadn't realised that. I'm sorry.

(*Pause.*)

TULLY: OK, then?

HAMILTON: Yes, I think so.

TULLY: From 'Grandam, one night . . .'
Fire away.

HAMILTON: 'Grandam, one night, as we did sit at supper,
My uncle –'

TULLY (*interrupting*): No, look, that's awful. You're so dreary. Sit up properly for a start and pull yourself together. That's better. – Now I don't see any indication in the text that York's meant to be a mournful little milksop. I'm sorry, I don't want to be too hard, but that's what you sound like. Give it more bounce, can't you? And cheer up. – And don't break it up so much. You've got to say 'Grandam' quite brightly, to sort of catch the old girl's attention – and believe me, it'll be wandering if you start like you did just now – do that, and then get on with it. (*Pause.*)

HAMILTON: 'Grandam, one night, as we did sit at supper,
My uncle Rivers talk'd how I did *grow*
More than my brother –'

TULLY (*interrupting*): No, that's not it. We've already *been* talking about how you grow more than your brother, so that's not the new point you want to make. We all know that Mummy and Granny have been talking about it. What York says is: 'That's funny, because *Uncle Rivers* was talking about that the other night, and *Uncle Gloster* said something quite different.' The uncles are the new factor; they're what you've got to underline. Right?

Pause.

HAMILTON: Tully, honestly – would you mind awfully – I think I'd rather not be in the play –

TULLY: No one's said you're going to be, have they?

HAMILTON: No, I mean, I'd rather not try.

TULLY: Shut up. 'Grandam, one night . . .'

HAMILTON: Please, Tully.

TULLY: Oh, for God's sake, get on, will you?

HAMILTON (*at the end of his resources*): 'Grandam, one night, as we did sit at supper,
My uncle Rivers talk'd how I did grow
More than my brother. "Ay," quoth my uncle Gloster,
"Small herbs have grace, great weeds –"'

TULLY (*interrupting*): Oh, no, look, that's hopeless. For Christ's sake use a bit of intelligence.

HAMILTON *dissolves into tears.*

Here we go. Come on, then, get it off your chest.

TULLY *is visibly embarrassed at this emotional development.*

Oh, look, I'm terribly sorry, but how was I to know you were so sensitive? – (*with interest*) Your specs are getting all steamed up.

HAMILTON *removes his spectacles, and drops them on the floor in the process.* TULLY *picks them up and throws them into his lap.*

Well, have you finished?

HAMILTON *resumes his spectacles, which he has dried.*

HAMILTON: I'm sorry. But there's no need to go on at me. I think you're the cruellest person I've ever met.

TULLY (*sympathetically*): I *know.* Isn't it awful?

HAMILTON: You can't expect me to be any good at this stuff.

TULLY: Then why did you come?

No answer to this.

I don't think there's any harm in being a bit cruel. You knew you were bad, didn't you, so why be shocked when I tell you so? If you're angry, why not be bloody rude, instead of flushing the cistern?

HAMILTON: I won't do it again.

TULLY: Hamilton, that's the first sensible thing you've said.

HAMILTON: Only I'm no good at being angry.

TULLY: I suppose you're too *nice.*

HAMILTON: Oh, shut up.

TULLY: That's better. Now say 'Go to hell, Tully!' Go on.

HAMILTON (*after a pause*): No.

TULLY: Why can't you be really bloody? Don't you wish you could?

HAMILTON: Of course I do. Only I can't think of anything to say back when people are foul to me. I mean, I'm not really clever, it'd be all right if I was. Then I could make them look stupid. But I don't think anyone's very frightened of me. They say I'm a drip, and I'm afraid they're right.

TULLY: Good lord, Hamilton, don't pity yourself all the time. You seem so determined to be ill-used. But you could hit them where it hurts if you wanted to. You say you're too dull, but you're too kind, too scrupulous – or too damned lazy, I don't know. – Look, surely you believe you're right and they're wrong, don't you?

HAMILTON: I suppose I do.

TULLY: Well, then, you must make them feel it. Not hide in a cupboard with your virtue going stale on you, just wishing to be left alone. I suppose you cherish all this nonsense about forgiving your enemies, too. I quite see one might respect them, but why forgive? What on earth are enemies for except to be beaten?

HAMILTON: I – I don't know.

TULLY: What about war?

HAMILTON: Oh, yes, war.

TULLY: Have you thought about that?

HAMILTON: Well, sort of.

TULLY: Sort of! You must have thought about it. Don't be silly.

HAMILTON: But war's silly, anyway, isn't it?

TULLY: War, *silly*? Are you mad? War's shattering, and ghastly, and maybe it's silly that wars are necessary – but how can you glibly call war itself *silly* – it beats me. God, your mind's like a bowl of bread and milk, a confusion of soggy little bits.

HAMILTON: I didn't mean –

TULLY: You didn't *think*. I suppose the whole idea of war is too beastly and rough for you. You react as the feeble always do to violence – you're scared stiff, but you prefer to say you're above it. Well, perhaps I oughtn't to destroy your illusions.

HAMILTON: I don't know, I mean, I never have fought or anything.

TULLY: Nor have I, you clown. I feel that war is something you should take an intelligent interest in, that's all. In fact war might do you the heck of a lot of good. You need to be under fire a bit, that's what you need.

HAMILTON: Are you sure?

TULLY: I'll tell you something, Hamilton. (*Pause.*) Once upon a time I met a German soldier at the Oval. He said it was a sort of sentimental pilgrimage. Apparently he ended the war as a prisoner there; funny place to keep prisoners, but still. Anyway, he told me more about war in an hour than I'd learnt in ten years. You see, he'd been in the retreat from Stalingrad before they moved him to the Western front. He was in a crack regiment, and they served the Nazis only in the certain hope of smashing them once the war was over.

But here were these brilliant, finely-trained men, stuck in a brutal situation, with wave after wave of Russians coming at them. You mowed them down and mowed them down, till your machine-gun was almost red-hot with firing, and you had to cool the parts in buckets of water. And then another wave of these mad Russians would come, roaring and howling, and you'd mow them down again, but of course every time some would get far enough to throw a grenade – and there'd be two or three of your men gone, and you knew *they'd* got thousands and thousands in reserve and could keep this up for weeks – and it goes on and on – you can't sleep or they'll overrun you.

Can you imagine the effect on a man? You know you're five times, ten times a better soldier than your enemy, but what if he comes at you thirty or forty to one? What can you do?

HAMILTON (*reasonably*): Run away.

TULLY: No! – Well, do you know what these poor Germans did? Between the Russian attacks, they sang, they did almost nothing else. Grim old ballads, songs about girls, hunting songs, drinking songs, hearty patriotic songs – someone, almost asleep, strumming at a guitar, and everyone else slumped around anyhow, singing, with the tears streaming down their faces –

HAMILTON: Tully?

TULLY: Yes?

HAMILTON: I hope you don't mind my interrupting, but was that a good thing?

TULLY: What?

HAMILTON: Them crying. You didn't think much of it when I cried.

TULLY: The circumstances were rather different. They were in a hopeless position, exhausted, humiliated, steadily being blasted out of existence –

HAMILTON: So was I!

TULLY (*laughing*): Hamilton!

There is almost a trace of affection in his voice. He removes it hastily.

No, the point is that war knocks the nonsense out of life. And when you know you're going to die, it sort of purifies you, as far as I can see. These men loved each other, Hamilton, I promise you, they loved each other with all their hearts, not because they felt they ought to, but because this love came weeping and laughing out of them, and because they had nothing else *left* to love, nothing in the whole wide world. And if some were old and some were young, or handsome, or ugly, it didn't matter. They embraced that human flesh because it was human. And it was war, Hamilton, silly war, that made them free. It never seems to happen when you're at peace.

HAMILTON (*after a pause*): You mean, because there's no-one to fight?

TULLY: Good lord, there are plenty, there are thousands. The only difference is, you have to unearth them for yourself, and that's not always easy. But at least it's better than being *told* who to fight, like you are in war – I mean, a nation, millions of people you've never even met. Makes it very nice and simple, of course, but that's where war's silly. I couldn't just go and shoot at complete strangers; they might be terribly nice people.

But peacetime, Hamilton – supposing in peacetime you could declare war on your own terms, against the civilian bullies and thieves and fakes, supposing you could take your time and pick them off quite cleanly, one by one, like a sort of celestial sniper, never hurting the nice people in the process – wouldn't you do it?

HAMILTON: Do you mean I should murder people?

TULLY: I don't see why not. If you're clever enough, of course.

HAMILTON: But how could you be sure who *was* bad?

TULLY: How can you be sure of anything? If you questioned every natural reaction, you couldn't walk, or breathe, even. I say it's pure cowardice not to do what you think's right.

HAMILTON: Somebody might think it was right to kill *you*.

TULLY: If they're acting from the courage of their convictions, I shan't argue.

HAMILTON: You wouldn't be there to argue! – Anyway, what about 'Thou shalt not kill'?

TULLY: Who says I shan't?

HAMILTON: The Bible.

TULLY: Which part? Who wrote it?

HAMILTON: I don't know.

TULLY: Someone who believed in Jehovah?

HAMILTON: God. Yes.

TULLY: Do you?

HAMILTON: Do I believe in God?

TULLY: Do you believe in God? I apologise for this old-fashioned conversation.

HAMILTON: Yes, I do.

TULLY: A good, kind, merciful God, of course.

HAMILTON: Yes.

TULLY: A sensible, decent God.

HAMILTON: Yes.

TULLY: Omnipotent, omniscient.

HAMILTON: Er – yes.

TULLY: And self-sufficient?

HAMILTON: Yes, I suppose so.

TULLY: Lacking nothing?

HAMILTON: Yes.

TULLY: Nothing?

HAMILTON: Yes. – No! – Yes!

TULLY: Then tell me why he made the world.

HAMILTON: Well, I suppose –

TULLY: For fun? He was bored?

HAMILTON: Oh, no. He made man in His own image, to love and praise Him.

TULLY: Hallelujah! So much for the God who lacked nothing. He lacked love, so he created a jolly little dog to lick Father's hand. But not to be fed very regularly.

HAMILTON: Oh, but surely –

TULLY: He was bored with his own company. He wanted to be admired. He wanted a waggly tail thumping by his fireside. I find your God almost human.

HAMILTON: Well, what's wrong with that?

TULLY: Think for a moment – I hope this isn't boring you too much, Hamilton? – think for a moment of the life of the average domestic dog. Think of some nice, devoted cocker spaniel. It has a proper basket; it's patted and made much of, lacks for nothing; it's sheltered from storm, plague and famine, and given the choicest scraps. Punishment is meted out with fairness, and received with cringing repentance and extravagant love. – This is sympathetically known as a Dog's Life, but it bears a wonderful resemblance to the theoretical life of a Christian.

HAMILTON: Oh, but, Tully –

TULLY: Now compare it with the *facts* of Man – the hard facts. Man is riddled with pain, want, grief, and frustrated desire. He's confused, discontented, and as a good, glossy tailwagger he's a prize flop. – Well, does this please God? Is this what he intended?

HAMILTON: No!

TULLY: Then let him do something about it, if he cares.

HAMILTON (*aghast*): Hey, Tully!

TULLY: Christ, you'll say next –

HAMILTON: He sent Christ down –

TULLY: To redeem it all. A last desperate gamble, not sparing his nearest and dearest. So what happens? A fine crop of martyrs, fanatics, neurotics, inquisitions and persecutions. Otherwise – nil. Mankind becoming more and more embarrassed and weepy, and incapable finally of loving even itself, never mind God. – And do you think the Old Boy's still got something up his sleeve? One last dead rabbit?

HAMILTON: But Christ has redeemed us –

TULLY: How absolutely splendid.

HAMILTON: This life is only to prepare for the next –

TULLY: Prep!

HAMILTON: We learn to love God.

TULLY: *Do* we? A God who won't admit he's made a mess of it? Determined we must love him if it kills us, too proud to call the whole thing off, although it's become a farce? Your God, Hamilton, this feeble old man? I prefer to believe in none.

HAMILTON (*wide-eyed with horror*): O God!

TULLY: You must speak up; he's rather deaf.

HAMILTON: God! God!

TULLY: He's on compassionate leave. Or just sulking. Let me try. – Look here, God, you blithering old fart, I say you're a fake, I say you don't exist. Would you mind giving us a definite answer, one way or the other?

HAMILTON: Oh, Tully, stop, don't!

TULLY: This lad here's getting in a muddle –

HAMILTON: Yes –

TULLY: Save his faith, God, there's a good chap. Or don't you think he's worth bothering about?

HAMILTON: I'm not, I'm not.

TULLY: If you're really there, could you manage to strike me dead, please, just to convince young Hamilton –

HAMILTON: No!

TULLY: If you've got the energy!

HAMILTON *hides his face in his hands, terrified. There is a long pause, during which* TULLY *is not struck dead.*

Don't worry, he hasn't. That God of yours is a master of turning the other cheek. – Hamilton, you have been praying to a phantom.

HAMILTON (*slowly raising his head*): No, not at all. It just shows how jolly merciful He is.

TULLY (*laughing*): Good try, child. – But no, come on – he's not there. Or if he is, he's not bothered with you. He wouldn't talk to you like I have. Look: I want you to be proud, and sufficient to yourself, and not cringe for favours, to God or to anyone. Do you promise?

HAMILTON: I promise.

TULLY (*with great gentleness*): It's better to be our own masters, really. I want you to stand on your own two feet: at least they're flesh and blood, not clay. Will you do it?

HAMILTON: I'm going to try.

TULLY: And care more about *this* life.

HAMILTON: Yes.

TULLY: And love the quick rather than the dead.

HAMILTON: Yes.

TULLY: And say 'No' sometimes.

HAMILTON (*smiling*): Yes.

TULLY: And now try Lady Anne.

HAMILTON: Phew! All right. Where from?

TULLY (*finding the place in* HAMILTON*'s book for him*): Here. Top of the page. I'll start. – Oh, this is where Lady Anne has a real go at Gloster for murdering her man. She's almost sure he did it. Gloster says Edward the Fourth did it. – I've marked in a few cuts. Can you follow them all right?

HAMILTON: Yes, thanks.

TULLY: Here goes, then:
'By such despair, I should accuse myself.
Say that I slew them not?'

HAMILTON (*with more feeling*): 'Why, then, they are not dead.'

TULLY: 'I did not kill your husband.'

HAMILTON: 'Why, then, he is alive.'

TULLY: 'Nay, he is dead, and slain by Edward's hand.'

HAMILTON: 'Thou wast provokèd by thy bloody mind,
That never dreamt on aught but butcheries.
Didst thou not kill this king?'

TULLY: 'I grant ye.'

HAMILTON: 'Dost grant me, hedgehog? Then God grant me too
Thou mayst be damnèd for that wicked deed!
O, he was gentle, mild and virtuous!'

TULLY: 'The fitter for the King of Heaven, that hath him.'

HAMILTON: 'And thou unfit for any place but hell.'

TULLY: 'Yes, one place else, if you will hear me name it.'

HAMILTON: 'Some dungeon.'

TULLY: 'Your bedchamber.'

There is a pause; something seems to be stifling HAMILTON.

HAMILTON: 'Ill rest betide the chamber where thou liest!'

TULLY: 'So will it, madam, till I lie with you.'

Long pause.

HAMILTON (*suddenly with quiet realism, in a still, small voice which is not Shakespeare's*): 'I hope so.'

TULLY (*echoing his tone*): 'I know so.'
(*Then, snapping back into the former idiom*)
'But, gentle Lady Anne,
Is not the causer of the timeless deaths
Of these Plantagenets, Henry and Edward,
As blameful as the executioner?'

HAMILTON: 'Thou was the cause and most accurs'd effect.'

TULLY: 'Your beauty was the cause of that effect;
Your beauty, that did haunt me in my sleep
To undertake the death of all the world' –

Then, quietly, not raising his eyes from the book.

Come to my room tonight.

HAMILTON (*with a start – apprehensive*): Tonight? – Why?

TULLY: You know where I sleep? The little room between the two upstairs dormitories?

HAMILTON: Yes, I know it. Goff used to be there when I was his fag. But –

TULLY: Come about half-past eleven.

HAMILTON: It's very kind of you, Tully, but I don't know.

TULLY: You must. Why not? Are you frightened?

HAMILTON: Well . . . yes.

TULLY: But it's as safe as houses. Ask Turner.

Pause. Each considers the implications of this remark.

HAMILTON: But . . . you see, I don't know what . . . I mean, what you'll want me to *do*. I'm afraid I'm awfully ignorant, I . . . well, I've been told about it by the Headmaster at my prep school, and my father, and Mr. Hallowes, but I don't know, it all seemed so . . . sort of vague. Something about the consummation of love – that's all I can remember. – And I hate not knowing what's going to happen. That frightens me more than anything. When I go to the dentist, I always make him tell me what he's doing all the time.

TULLY: That's a flattering comparison. Look, I won't hurt you and I won't laugh at you. OK?

HAMILTON: Yes, but – well, what happens?

TULLY: Think of yourself as milk over a slow flame. The warmth of the bed, the excitement of being held and caressed by another body, begins to bring you to the boil. You simmer and tingle, and all over you there's this longing to be relieved of a huge burden of love that's climbing up through your body. The surface of the milk bumps and flickers, and then slowly, and then faster and faster, so that you can hardly bear it, it rises up, and at last there's a long moment of perfect suspense, and you boil over – and that, Hamilton – that's all there is to it. – Well, what do you say?

HAMILTON (*resolutely*): All right. I don't know what you're talking about, but OK.

Pause.

TULLY: Good boy. And suppose you regret it?

HAMILTON: I won't regret it, Tully.

TULLY: You won't.

HAMILTON: I shall be completely in your power. I shall have to trust you.

TULLY (*after a pause*): And I you. If you betray me . . . but you won't.

HAMILTON: No.

A knock on the door.

TULLY: Damn. Come in!

Enter TURNER.

TURNER: Tully – oh, sorry. I didn't realise you were auditioning.

TULLY: Who told you I was?

TURNER: Oh, well, I – hm! Sorry I disturbed you.

TULLY: Don't mention it.

TURNER: The laundry's being collected. Which of the shirts are to go?

TULLY: Hang on a second. – Hamilton, I think you've given me a fair taste of your quality. Read the play right through, if you can, in the next day or two. And you know when to come?

HAMILTON: Yes, Tully.

TULLY: Good. And – Hamilton – you did very well, you know.

HAMILTON (*modestly*): Oh – thank you.

(*Exit.*)

TURNER (*salaciously*): Well – ripe for shaking?

TULLY (*suddenly quite exhausted*): The shirt will do for tomorrow. But send those flannels, they're a bit green about the knees.

TURNER: Don't worry; they went half an hour ago. – Now, come on, how did it go?

TULLY: We talked.

TURNER: You mean *you* talked. What else? He didn't look as sleepy as usual.

TULLY: He isn't sleepy. I like him.

TURNER: Well, you see, he's not so bad really. Bit of a drip, but not so bad.

TULLY (*annoyed*): Anyone who doesn't chatter like you is a drip, naturally.

TURNER: You feel sorry for him.

TULLY: I certainly don't.

TURNER: Then what do you feel?

Pause.

TULLY: Ashamed. And cheap. – Now shut up.

TURNER (*after a moment*): Well – when?

TULLY: Tonight.

TURNER: Gosh (*Pause.*) I should think he'll pass out during breakfast tomorrow and go flop in the porridge.

TULLY (*coldly*): I don't think so.

TURNER (*rapt*): Gosh.

Pause.

TULLY: Look, go and see to the laundry, will you, there's a good lad.

TURNER: But it's gone – I told you.

TULLY (*insistent*): Go and see to it.

Pause.

TURNER (*unhappily*): All right. I'm sorry.

Exit. TULLY still seems exhausted and in a dream. Mechanically he picks up the large Shakespeare which HAMILTON had used, and begins to read in it. Then, suddenly, he smiles to himself – almost laughs – slams it shut, and is putting it back on the shelf as

The curtain slowly falls.

ACT THREE

Scene One

TULLY's *study. It is Sunday morning, four days later.*

TULLY *is trying, not altogether successfully, to oil his cricket bat without oiling his Sunday suit as well. TURNER, holding two pairs of* TULLY's *shoes, is spluttering with indignation.*

TURNER: Well, honestly, crumbs, I do think it's the bloody limit, quite frankly.

TULLY: I've said I'm sorry, Tich.

TURNER: Fat lot of good that does. I mean, I don't understand what you see in him.

TULLY: How could you possibly? Anyway, who started the whole thing?

TURNER: I know, don't rub it in. *Peccavi.*

TULLY: On the contrary, you never did a better thing. I shan't forget it.

TURNER: Nor shall I.

TULLY: Look, it may be your fault, or mine, but it's certainly not his, so you've nothing to hold against him. You acted from the worst possible motives, and it happens to have been an inspiration.

TURNER: I suppose you're in love or something wet.

TULLY: God knows.

TURNER (*singing*): 'I'm in love, I'm in love, I'm in love with a wonderful drip!'

TULLY (*roaring*): Shut up!

Abruptly, the door is thrown open and PARK comes in, scowling and melodramatic.

PARK: Oh – Turner, would you mind just clearing out for a minute.

TURNER: Yes, Park. Certainly, Park. (*To TULLY, indicating the shoes*) I'll get these done right away.

TULLY: Thanks.

Exit TURNER.

PARK (*furious*): Well, congratulations!

TULLY: What?

PARK: I congratulate you.

TULLY: Very decent of you. May one know why?

PARK: I'm afraid you won't laugh your way out of this. I saw Hamilton coming out of your room this morning at about six o'clock. I was on my way to the bog and I thought I heard talking in the upstairs dormitories. But it wasn't in the dormitories, it was in your room, and while I was watching, Hamilton came out. – It hasn't taken me long to realise what it means.

TULLY (*looking at his watch*): It's taken you six and a quarter hours.

PARK: I ought to smash you.

TULLY: I shouldn't try. – Look, Mungo, this is rather silly. Tell me what's biting you, for God's sake, and try to make it sound like sense.

PARK: I said I saw Hamilton coming out of your room.

TULLY: Odd that I didn't.

PARK: I suppose I was seeing visions.

TULLY: Not a vision that does you much credit.

PARK: Or you.

TULLY: You're really serious? You saw Hamilton – of all people –

PARK: I saw him.

TULLY: I suppose he must sleepwalk or something.

PARK: Can't you do better than that?

TULLY: Well, for God's sake, why didn't you accuse him on the spot, if you really thought something was up?

PARK: Because it didn't strike me at once, that's why. It had never occurred to me that you, of all people –

TULLY: But I gather it occurs now.

PARK: Yes, it damned well does.

TULLY: It's your word against mine.

PARK: Look, I wouldn't have made this up, would I? You had Hamilton with you last night. Are you going on denying it?

TULLY (*with a sigh*): All right, Mungo. Sorry. Yes, Hamilton was with me; has been for the last four nights. I haven't enjoyed the deception, you know, but with your attitude, what else could I do?

PARK: Look here –

TULLY: Don't let it worry you. It's perfectly honourable.

PARK: Huh! Like hell it is.

TULLY: Does Hamilton strike you as a vicious type?

PARK: I wouldn't have guessed he was a tart.

TULLY (*grimly*): I should mind what you're saying, Mungo.

PARK: I'm not very interested in your finer feelings for Hamilton. They don't seem to make much difference to what happens in the end. Still, they may impress the Old Man.

TULLY: Quite seriously, you know, I think they would.

PARK: Well, we'll soon see.

TULLY: How do you mean? – Does he know?

PARK: No, but he will in a minute.

TULLY (*slowly*): You wouldn't do that.

PARK: I can't hush it up just because you happen to have been a friend of mine.

TULLY: Oh, we're in the past tense. Well. I think that's a pity.

PARK (*sanctimoniously*): Look, John, I couldn't let you go on with that sort of thing. It's a death-trap. What I'm doing is the best for both of you in the long run. I know this sounds pompous, but – you'll thank me one day.

TULLY (*bitterly*): Not today, though. As if you needed thanks. Oh, go and do your duty, old pal. I know it hurts you much more than it hurts me.

PARK: A fine friend you've been.

TULLY: Well, I was fond of you. I'd never have turned you over to the cops.

PARK: Don't try and put me in the wrong. You've got too much ground to make up. – I'm going now.

TULLY: Go on, then, you splendid fellow.

Exit PARK. *After a few moments,*
TULLY *goes to the door, opens it and
shouts* Fag! *Feet are heard running up.*

Is Hamilton there? – Oh, Hamilton,
come in here a moment, will you?
There are some changes in rehearsal
times that affect you. – All right, you
others.

Enter HAMILTON. TULLY *shuts the
door.*

We've had it, Tim. Park saw you
coming out of my room this morning.

HAMILTON (*who seems to have gained
in confidence since we last saw him*):
Oh, crikey, I'm sorry. I did bump into
him, but I said I'd taken the wrong way
to the rears by mistake, and he seemed
to believe me. Has he changed his
mind?

TULLY: He certainly has.

HAMILTON: Is it serious?

TULLY: Couldn't be much worse. I don't
know what the hell I can say. The Old
Man's going to be shaken rigid – one of
his trusted Prefects.

HAMILTON (*astonished*): You mean
Park's going to *tell* him? But, John, I
thought he was a friend of yours.

TULLY: So did I. Apparently this is
Bigger than Both of Us. Well, we must
just deny it.

HAMILTON: He won't believe us, will
he? Let's tell the truth, John, it's
simpler.

TULLY: Look, it's curtains for me if we
do, and it wouldn't help your prospects
much.

HAMILTON: We had to take the risk,
didn't we? It can't be helped.

TULLY: It must be helped. You must
think up some stories about sleep-
walking. At least Park didn't actually
catch us together, that's something. –
Hell, this would happen. I'm terribly
sorry.

HAMILTON: I'm not going to whine
about it, so don't you start!

TULLY (*beating his brow*): Damn, I can't
think straight, just when I need to.
What am I going to say? I'll never
convince the Old Man that Park's
lying. Everyone knows he's incapable

of it. – Why the hell wasn't I more
careful? – Look, we must stick together,
whatever happens, we mustn't tell
different stories. Will the sleep-walking
be any good?

HAMILTON: I never have sleep-walked.

TULLY: You're a lot of help.

HAMILTON: John, let's tell the truth.

TULLY: No.

HAMILTON: We'll have to in the end.

TULLY: Why should we? He's not likely
to torture us. No, we must say we're
innocent, and stick to it.

HAMILTON: Well, we *are* innocent. Not
of what Park's saying, but, I mean,
we've done nothing wrong. It didn't *feel*
wrong. I'd have *felt* if it had been.

TULLY: I know, but you mustn't say that
to Hallowes, for God's sake.

HAMILTON: Won't he understand?

TULLY: Of course he won't – You were
sleep-walking, remember.

HAMILTON (*laughing*): But it's silly, it's
obvious! Even I can see that.

TULLY: You do as I say, and don't be
scared.

HAMILTON: I'm not! Well, I mean, I
am, but I'm not going to say anything
silly.

TULLY: I hope not. You were *sleep-
walking*. – Oh, damn and blast!

HAMILTON: Funny, I'd have thought
you'd rather enjoy a situation like this.

TULLY: *Enjoy* it!

HAMILTON: All I wish is –

Enter PARK.

TULLY (*angry*): It would be nice if you
could knock. This *is* my study, not
yours.

PARK: You're here, are you, Hamilton?
What a coincidence. Well, you'd better
stay here, now, till you're wanted. (*To*
TULLY) He wants to see you straight
away. Come on.

HAMILTON: Good luck.

TULLY: Thank you, Tim. Same to you.

Exeunt PARK *and* TULLY.

Curtain

Scene Two

HALLOWES's *study, immediately afterwards.*

HALLOWES *is at his desk. There is a knock at the door.*

HALLOWES: Come in.

Enter PARK, *followed by* TULLY.

PARK: Here's Tully, sir.

HALLOWES: All right, Park. Keep an eye on Hamilton, will you? And bring him along in about ten minutes. He can wait outside till I'm ready.

PARK: Yes, sir. (*Exit.*)

TULLY *is doing a good imitation of a man in a daze.*

HALLOWES: Well, Tully, what have you got to say about this?

TULLY: I hardly know what to say, sir. It's so incredible.

HALLOWES: You deny what Park says, then?

TULLY: I should think I *do*, sir. I don't understand what it's all about.

HALLOWES: You do know what Park's told me, I imagine?

TULLY: Well, he said something about me and Hamilton.

HALLOWES: He says he saw Hamilton coming from your room early this morning. Is that true, Tully?

TULLY: No, sir, it is not. – To my knowledge, at least.

HALLOWES: Yet I don't feel Park would make it up.

TULLY: Nor do I, sir. It beats me.

HALLOWES: Yes. Do you think he can have made a mistake?

TULLY: Well, I don't know, sir. It wouldn't be like him. I don't know. When did he say he saw Hamilton?

HALLOWES: I think he said about six o'clock.

TULLY: Yes, I see.

HALLOWES: And you know nothing about it?

TULLY: Nothing at all, sir, I'm sorry. Has Park asked Hamilton about it?

What does *he* say?

HALLOWES: No, I don't think Hamilton's been questioned yet. Indeed, I hope not. According to Park, when Hamilton saw him he said: 'I'm sorry, Park, I went the wrong way,' and Park just said: 'All right, then; get back to bed.'

TULLY: He didn't accuse him of anything?

HALLOWES: Apparently not.

TULLY: Sir, why on earth didn't he come straight in and see me about it, if he had any doubts?

HALLOWES: Well, I don't know; I asked him that. I gather it was for a variety of reasons; he wasn't quite sure of himself, I think, he thought perhaps he ought to consult me first – and besides, he found it hard to suspect one of his own friends.

TULLY: Well, I wish he had said something. I mean, this is nasty.

HALLOWES: Can you give me any proof that Park's wrong?

TULLY: Well, no, sir, I was asleep when this happened. I don't know about Hamilton. He may be able to throw some light on it, I suppose he was going to the rears and wandered down the wrong way. It could happen.

HALLOWES: How do you think he came to be down by your room, though?

TULLY: I suppose he missed the passage and took the next turning instead. One's so dopey at that time of morning, it'd be easy enough to do. And the door of my room would roughly correspond to where the door should have been. – Did Park ask him if he'd been in my room, sir?

HALLOWES: I don't think so, no. You mean it might not even have been your room?

TULLY: I don't know, sir. It's odd he didn't wake me up, because I *am* rather a light sleeper.

HALLOWES: Yes. What's the next door?

TULLY: The linen cupboard.

HALLOWES: Yes. I can't imagine that he was sleep-walking.

TULLY: No, sir, it doesn't sound like it.

HALLOWES: The thing is, Tully, Park is quite certain he heard voices down in your direction.

TULLY: Oh. Well, I dare say if Hamilton *did* come into my room, he probably apologised on the way out, in case I was awake.

HALLOWES: All the more surprising if you'd slept through it.

TULLY: Yes, sir, quite true.

HALLOWES: And Park says he heard two voices.

TULLY: Does he, sir?

HALLOWES: Yes. How would you account for that?

TULLY: I don't know, sir. All I feel is, with Park and Hamilton both wandering about half-asleep wanting to be excused, it all seems so vague. And why Park should decide to try and pin this thing on me – I don't get it.

HALLOWES: Tully, I want you to tell me the truth. Did you have Hamilton with you last night?

TULLY: No, sir. I didn't.

Pause.

HALLOWES: I'm sorry, Tully, but I don't believe you.

TULLY: Sir – surely! Why? – Oh, I know you might suspect me – these artistic types, and so on – but Hamilton – surely not, sir! I mean, rather a quiet, shy sort of studious little boy like that – it's so improbable. I'd say Hamilton was about as innocent as they came.

HALLOWES: Innocents are easy dupes, you know.

TULLY: Well, sir, *I* haven't duped him!

HALLOWES (*after a pause*): I'm glad to hear it. – What *have* you done to him, Tully?

TULLY (*beginning to be seriously rattled*): Nothing, sir. I don't know anything about him.

HALLOWES: Except that he's innocent.

TULLY: Well – yes.

HALLOWES: He won't get punished. You needn't worry about that. I believe in his innocence too.

TULLY: Punished for what?

HALLOWES: Tully, this is rather pathetic, you know.

Long pause.

TULLY: All right, sir. I'm sorry.

HALLOWES: Park told me you had admitted it.

TULLY: I thought he must have done.

HALLOWES: I wish you could have spared me the lies.

TULLY: Yes, sir.

HALLOWES: Well, what was Hamilton doing in your room?

TULLY: He spent the night with me. I asked him to.

HALLOWES: Was it the first time?

TULLY: No, sir, the fourth.

HALLOWES (*somewhat taken aback*): You don't seem to feel any shame for what you've done. You seem almost proud.

TULLY: I'm *not* proud, sir, honestly. And certainly not ashamed. Sack me, but don't ask me to say it was wrong.

HALLOWES: My dear fellow, don't be stubborn about it. You tried to defend Hamilton, and I give you some credit for that. But if you'd really felt any affection for the boy, the last thing you'd have wanted would be to do what you did.

TULLY: Sir, don't make me tell you what I felt for him. I don't want to discuss it. All I'll say is that I've had plenty of boys to bed with me here, and not cared a button for one of them. But with Hamilton, it was extraordinary – I found I cared so much, I was almost tempted not to lay a finger on him, just as a sort of tribute.

HALLOWES: Tully, you are incredible. I'm trying to understand and make allowances, but it's very hard when you seem so thoroughly smug about corrupting him – and others, apparently.

TULLY: Sir, that isn't true. I *haven't* corrupted him.

HALLOWES: You were out for what you could get. You didn't care what you did to him.

TULLY: Sir, I swear I did. You could have said that in any other case and I shouldn't have argued – but not in this. – All I say is, look at Hamilton, and see if he isn't more alive, more of a person than he was a week ago. I don't guarantee that his cricket will improve, but at least he can stick up for himself. – Oh, sir, if that's corruption, you ought to encourage it, surely.

HALLOWES: Redemption through vice is an old heresy, Tully, and it hasn't worn well. What do you suppose a few hours of smut with you are likely to bring out in a boy like Hamilton – except possibly a taste for smut?

TULLY: If that was all it was, I wouldn't bother to defend it.

HALLOWES: Now look here, Tully. If we've got to part company, I should like us to part as friends. I hold no brief for what you've done, and nor do you, in your own heart. You know it was wrong as well as I do. But what shocks me almost more than that, is the degree of hypocrisy you've been practising on me, on Park, and all of us.

TULLY: Surely, sir, I've been as unhypocritical as I could be in the circumstances. You never found me raising a moral stink like Park.

HALLOWES: My dear Tully, if I were accusing you of keeping a brothel, it would be irrelevant for you to point out that the accounts had been kept with scrupulous fairness. Why bother to defend your integrity?

TULLY: Because, well, you seem more hurt about my letting you down than about the thing I've done.

HALLOWES: Believe me, Tully that is absolutely unfair. There's no comparison between the two things. But surely you can understand that after twenty-five years as a schoolmaster, I'm more likely to be shocked by calculated deceit than by mere physical weakness.

TULLY: Yes, sir, I see that. But this physical weakness – why do you call it weakness when it seems more like a kind of strength? I tell you, I *can't* feel guilt for what I've done with Hamilton. I honestly can't. It's just as if you were to show me, oh, a ripe apple, or a warm fresh loaf, and tell me they were foul and disgusting. I shouldn't believe you.

And it's the same with this. Everything in me, honestly, my conscience and my heart and mind and everything, says it's *right*. I *know* it is – I'm not fooling myself, I'm not trying to smother my better nature. There's no sort of angry little voice buried away in a dungeon, howling at the back of it that it's wrong. How can it be wrong? What possible harm can it do us or anyone else?

HALLOWES: I don't say it will leave any permanent effects if we behave sensibly about it.

TULLY: No, you're still treating it as a mishap. Tell me why it should be. You say yourself that these relationships are natural at school.

HALLOWES: *Attraction* I said was natural. Affection. Not physical contact.

TULLY: But, sir, you can't say desire was given us only to increase the birth-rate.

HALLOWES: That is its primary function.

TULLY: Yes, but there's rather a generous supply of encouragement, isn't there? It's not all needed to produce babies, so why restrict the surplus to women? Especially when there aren't any about.

HALLOWES: It's not something you can argue. It's a simple matter of instinct.

TULLY (*warming to the argument*): Oh, but, sir, instinct's such a toss-up, isn't it, really? I mean, look at Polynesian natives and people. It's just the convention you were brought up in. Or else a personal reaction, like a stomach that throws up lobster. – Still, we don't disagree as much as we seem to, sir. We both believe that goodness is good, and badness is bad. That's something, isn't it?

HALLOWES: My dear Tully, your goodness is personal taste, rooted in nothing. You have put poison in Hamilton's mind.,

TULLY (*firmly*): No. sir.

HALLOWES: You have done a very horrible thing.

Pause.

TULLY: Do you really think it's so horrible, sir?

HALLOWES: Why –

TULLY (*breaking in*): Sir – can I speak quite frankly to you?

HALLOWES: You know you can.

TULLY: Well, sir – would you feel horror if you were in bed with a boy – Hamilton, for instance?

Pause.

HALLOWES: The case would never arise.

TULLY: No, I know. But the thought – you can imagine it, sir? Does it fill you with loathing?

HALLOWES: No. Not with loathing. No human being fills me with that.

TULLY: Physical revulsion, then?

HALLOWES: No. There is nothing unclean in the human body. A boy's body can be a supremely beautiful thing. Of course it can.

TULLY: And I couldn't resist taking it in my arms. Do you blame me for that?

HALLOWES (*with an effort*): Of course I'm not *blaming* you, my dear boy. It's not for us to blame people for weaknesses. What I do blame you for is not even having *wished* to resist it.

TULLY: But I knew there was no harm –

HALLOWES: How can you say you *knew*?

TULLY: And when you come down to it, sir – what do you find *wrong* in the thing itself? – putting aside the question of younger boys for the moment –

HALLOWES: All right – for the moment.

TULLY: Suppose it's between two boys of the same age, who aren't virgins, and there's no question of influencing – would you call it a bad thing – in itself?

HALLOWES (*after a moment's hesitation*): But you carefully put aside the vital point – the effect on the younger boy. You've got to shoulder that; every act has its consequence. You can't pretend Hamilton was equally responsible for what happened between you. You used persuasion.

TULLY: Well –

HALLOWES: You prevailed upon him, knowing very well how powerless he was against you. That's a terrible and cruel thing to do.

TULLY: But you talk as if I'd somehow overpowered him –

HALLOWES: Of course you overpowered him – your intellect, your age, your physical advantage. He had no choice.

TULLY: He had a choice, and he chose to do it.

HALLOWES (*grimly*): You certainly show no inclination to shoulder the blame, Tully.

TULLY: Oh, lord, sir, I wasn't meaning that.

HALLOWES: I'm glad to hear it.

TULLY: You mustn't punish him, sir. Not that I admit that there's anything to punish, but in any case I'm responsible.

HALLOWES: Indeed you are. For forcing him to take the part of a woman, for your personal gratification.

TULLY: That isn't true.

HALLOWES: It is true, and I find it unforgivable. Surely you know the sort of pathetic half-men that are the logical development of that situation – men with painted faces and womanish gestures? I've seen them, if you haven't. Ruined human lives, a misery to themselves and a joke to others. Suppose in ten years' time Hamilton were to be like that – could you forgive yourself?

TULLY (*angry, almost shouting*): No, I couldn't. But he won't be. He's more of a man than he was, not less.

HALLOWES: Was he manly when he submitted to you? Really, Tully!

TULLY (*furious*): Why do you assume that every sexual act must have a male and a female to it?

HALLOWES: But naturally it does –

TULLY (*raging on*): For that matter, why shouldn't he be the active one and me the passive? Well, if you want to know, when Hamilton and I lie together, there's no submitting, there's no top dog and substitute bitch –

HALLOWES: Tully, I'm not a bit interested –

TULLY: No, you'd rather shut your eyes and assume it to be horrible. How can you be fair if you won't look?

HALLOWES: You can lecture me if it makes you feel better, Tully.

TULLY: I'm sorry. But, sir, what are you going to do with Hamilton?

HALLOWES: Help him, that's all I can do. There's a lot to put right.

TULLY: I don't like the sound of that much, sir.

HALLOWES (angry at last): It's not very important what you like. You've done enough for that boy. You've played your part; you have no more concern in him. He stays; you go.

TULLY: I'm glad he can stay, anyway. – Or am I? I don't mind you poisoning his mind against me – well, I mean, I do mind, like hell, but I suppose it can't be helped. But poisoning him right through, teaching him to be meek and long-suffering again – you can't, you can't –

HALLOWES: I can, and with God's grace I will.

TULLY: Oh, naturally, God is your ally. I fully expect a cohort of angels to help you to crush our puny rebellion.

HALLOWES: You try to make yourself sound very sympathetic. Rebellion! A systematic cheapening of others' values by contagion with your own.

TULLY: Ah, the good old party line –

HALLOWES: There is only one thing for you to do – clear out of his life, and don't try to interfere with it again. Not that I imagine your interest in his mind will survive long after you lose control of his body.

TULLY: That is a foul thing to say!

HALLOWES: I know you admire plain speaking.

TULLY: Yes, when it has some regard for the truth.

HALLOWES (blazing): Your regard for yourself overrides everything. – I don't think there's any point in going on with this. – If you had been truly fond of the boy, and had given way to a stupid impulse, and were sorry for it – I could understand, at least. I should do all I could to help you, and see if the whole thing couldn't be got harmlessly over somehow or other. Believe me, that was my first reaction when Park told me what he knew. – But as you clearly have no shame and no regret for what you've done, I can't find it in me to sympathise with you. I'm afraid there's no place for you in this house, and you needn't expect sympathy from the Headmaster. You will go home as soon as you've packed, and in the meantime I shall ring up your parents. You will discuss it with nobody, is that understood? – Now, I asked Park to bring Hamilton along. Will you see if he's there?

TULLY goes to the door and opens it, letting in HAMILTON.

Hamilton, Tully will be leaving tomorrow.

TULLY shrugs at HAMILTON and tries to look reassuring.

All right, Tully. You can go.

Exit TULLY.

Sit down, Hamilton.

HAMILTON sits.

Now, I want you to know that I'm truly sorry for your part in this business. I'm going to try and make it as easy for you as I can. What you can do for me is not to be frightened, but to make a clean breast of what's happened. Will you do that?

HAMILTON: Yes, sir, that's what I want to do.

Slow curtain

Scene Three

TULLY's study, a few minutes later.

TURNER is beginning to pack TULLY's belongings in a trunk.

TURNER: You won't want all these books packed, will you? School ones, I mean.

TULLY: Lord, no. You can have those.

TURNER: Oh, but I've got plenty –

TULLY: Sell 'em back, and you'll get a few bob.

TURNER: Oh, thanks. Thanks awfully.

He picks out TULLY's *pocket edition of* Richard III *from the school books.*

You want *Richard III* to go too?

TULLY (*taking it from him*): No, better keep that. It has its place in my career.

TURNER: Damned shame about the play. – Gosh, it's all jolly sudden, isn't it?

TULLY: Certainly is.

TURNER: Had you imagined it happening?

TULLY (*taking a pair of candlesticks from the mantelpiece*): These any use to you?

TURNER: Well –

TULLY: You can always flog them.

TURNER (*accepting them*): Yes. Thanks. – Had you?

TULLY: Had I what?

TURNER: Thought of this happening?

TULLY: Well, of course; don't be a clot. There's always the risk.

TURNER: Yes.

TULLY: There was with you and me.

TURNER (*it had never really struck him*): I suppose there was. It seems worse, though, happening to someone like Crab.

TULLY: I never expected you to be so sympathetic.

He takes down the guitar from the wall and hands it to TURNER.

Here.

TURNER (*delighted*): Oh, no, honestly, you –

TULLY: I'm not *giving* it to you. Pack it.

TURNER: Oh. Sorry. Yes.

TULLY: Put plenty of socks and things round it.

TURNER: If it won't mind the stink. (*He begins to cope with it.*)

TULLY *looks on with misgivings.*

TULLY: No, not that way up, look –

(*intervening*) oh, it had better go separately. (*He lays it aside.*)

TURNER: Crab'll be OK, won't he? I mean, he'll only be having a talking-to?

TULLY: That's all.

TURNER: The Old Man would never expel him.

TULLY: Good lord, no. He said he wasn't going to.

TURNER: Crab being the innocent party.

TULLY: The Old Man has strong views on innocence. The younger partner is always innocent.

TURNER: Well, in this case, he was, wasn't he?

TULLY: Depends what you call innocent. He chose to do what he did.

TURNER: Well, yes, but under pressure.

TULLY: He chose. That was the whole point.

TURNER: But whose idea was it?

TULLY: Yours, as a matter of fact.

TURNER: Oh, gosh, so it was. – Well, as long as you didn't shoot that line at the Old Man.

TULLY: About it being your idea?

TURNER: No, I mean about Crab choosing it. (*Pause.*) Did you?

TULLY: I said he had a mind of his own. I mean, he's not in his pram.

TURNER: But you took all the blame.

TULLY: Of course I did.

Pause.

TURNER: Still, I don't see why you had to insist on Crab being a free thinker.

TULLY: I said he did what he thought right. He wasn't a victim.

TURNER: Well, but look, if he's innocent, he *is* a victim. It's dangerous for him if you say he wasn't, whatever you may think –

TULLY: What the hell do you know about it?

TURNER: I dare say he *was* free, but you should have kept quiet about it for his sake.

TULLY (*angered*): Oh, dry up.

TURNER: I was only saying –

TULLY (*roaring*): Well, don't! I'm not supposed to be discussing all this, you know. (*Silence.*) The raincoat can go on top. (*Silence.*) The Old Man's convinced of his purity, anyway.

TURNER: Crab's?

TULLY: Yes. Convinced.

TURNER: I suppose he'll let him see you before you go?

TULLY: Oh, I'm sure he will. He's humane, if nothing else.

TURNER: And then I suppose you go home.

TULLY: That's right.

TURNER: It's going to be deadly here without you, honestly. And Park doesn't leave for *two more terms*! I don't know how we'll stick it. He's been Head of House for *ages*, hasn't he?

TULLY: He rose to office very young. Moral scrum-halves usually do. – Come on, we're not getting anywhere. Better start on the tuck-box. Bring it over.

TURNER *drags the tuck-box into the centre.*

I hereby bequeath to you – (*he produces them from the box*) – two tins of sardines – mushroom soup – one large and one small baked beans –

TURNER: How nice. Are they friends?

TULLY: Hush, Park may be listening.

TURNER (*fiercely, glaring into the tuck-box*): Where is Park? Which is he? Oh, look – (*he takes out a small package*) – here's Park, this nasty little square thing wrapped in white paper – (*he puts the package on the floor*) – that is Park –

TULLY: That is plum-cake.

TURNER: – and this is Turner! (*He jumps viciously on the package, squashing it flat.*) Bloody Park! (*He jumps again and again, then stops abruptly.*) Did you say it was plum-cake?

TULLY: Yes.

TURNER: Oh, dear. Oh, what a pity.

TULLY: Never mind, it served its purpose. – Now: a tin of apricots, a tin of condensed milk, and – and I don't know what this one is. The label's gone. Brown Windsor, probably.

TURNER (*shaking it critically*): I think it's gooseberries. – John, how will you – well, I mean, are you going to see Crab in the hols., or what?

TULLY: I expect so.

TURNER: Of course, you won't be able to write to him here, because the Old Man and Park will be keeping their eyes skinned for your postmark. Look – send his letters to me, and I'll pass them on.

TULLY: Thanks. That's a good idea.

TURNER: I suppose you can't have him to stay in the hols., if your parents know – unless they're very uncommon parents.

TULLY: They aren't.

TURNER: No, well, then, you'll have to organise the thing in style. I think you ought to arrange to meet at some incredibly picturesque little pub in some really stunning bit of country –

TULLY: Penge.

TURNER: No, but – oh, honestly, rise to the occasion, can't you? You've been sacked, it's all terribly dramatic, Crab is left behind to continue his Rake's Progress –

TULLY: That'll do.

TURNER: No, actually, that's rather important, isn't it? I mean, he's bound to have lots more sex here.

TULLY: I shouldn't think so.

TURNER: Why, do you think it would be bad for him?

TULLY: I don't know.

TURNER: It hasn't done you much harm, has it?

TULLY: I don't think so. More good, if anything.

TURNER (*with conviction*): Same here. It passes, anyway, doesn't it?

TULLY: Supposed to, yes.

TURNER: But, well, I've heard of people getting stuck with it.

TULLY: I think they might if they'd wanted it at school and not had it.

TURNER (*happily*): Then we're all right, Jack! *And* Crab, thanks to timely work by the Salvation Army. – Shall I send you sort of Gestapo reports on his behaviour? The frustrated types are always the worst once they've broken their duck.

TULLY (*furious*): Shut up, will you? What a stinking little mind you've got!

TURNER: Why, don't you want him to be a credit to you?

TULLY: No, I don't! Not in that way.

TURNER: I must say you're a great bundle of fun today. – Still, you have been sacked.

A clock strikes outside.

TULLY: Hell, how long's he been in there? It seems ages.

TURNER: Only a few minutes.

TULLY (*suddenly alarmed*): Suppose the Old Man isn't going to let me see him –

TURNER: You know he will.

TULLY: But suppose he doesn't. Suppose he keeps him there all day, or something. What the hell can we do?

TURNER: Go in with them thar guns blazin', and carry him out. Soon be lunch-time anyway.

TULLY: But seriously –

There is a knock on the door.

Come in!

Enter HAMILTON.

God, what a relief! We were just coming in with a posse.

TURNER: We were going to brain the Old Man with a squash racket.

TULLY: Was he decent about it?

HAMILTON: Oh, yes, he was all right. He talked about you, mostly.

TULLY (*interested*): Did he? What did he say?

HAMILTON: He didn't seem too keen on you.

TULLY: I gathered that when I saw him.

What else?

HAMILTON: He said you were entirely to blame. I said that was silly –

TULLY: I said that too –

HAMILTON (*not altogether pleased*): Did you? Oh.

TULLY: Well, I mean, I said you had a will of your own.

TURNER: Dead thoughtful, the boy.

TULLY (*to* TURNER): Shut up. (*To* HAMILTON) Anyway, that didn't shake his faith in you? There was no question of expulsion or anything?

HAMILTON: Oh – er – no, nothing like that.

TULLY: Oh, good, well, that's OK, then.

TURNER: He's not a bad old sausage, really. He means jolly well.

HAMILTON (*laughing*): Yes.

TURNER: I knew he wouldn't want you to go.

TULLY: He didn't even mention it?

HAMILTON: No, not really.

TULLY: Well, did he?

HAMILTON: Er, no – no.

TULLY (*sensing something wrong*): Look, it really is all right, isn't it?

HAMILTON *does not look up.*

Hey. It is all right, isn't it? (*Silence.*) Don't be a clown. What's wrong?

TURNER: Come on, Crab.

HAMILTON: Nothing's wrong . . . but I'm leaving.

TURNER: You're – oh, funny joke.

HAMILTON: I am, actually.

TURNER: No, seriously.

HAMILTON: I am serious.

TULLY (*speaking at last*): You are?

HAMILTON *nods.*

What do you mean? Why? Do you mean he *did* sack you?

HAMILTON: No.

TULLY: Then – Tim, what on earth are you blathering about?

HAMILTON: I told him I didn't want to stay.

TURNER: You are joking, Crab, aren't you?

HAMILTON (*patiently*): No. He didn't want to sack me, but he said he'd sacked John, so I said I was going too.

TULLY (*after a pause*): Look, it's awfully nice of you, but you're crackers. Of course you mustn't leave; that's ridiculous. Why do you want to leave?

HAMILTON: I think I ought to.

TULLY: You mean you want to do the 'decent thing', and take your share of the blame.

HAMILTON: It's not that.

TULLY: Well, what *are* you trying to do?

TURNER: Crab, look, you *can't* leave. It's all right for this old horror, he's eighteen, he's finished anyway, it'll hardly be noticed. But being sacked at fourteen – well, leaving at fourteen – that's a bit steep. I mean, if you *want* to leave under a cloud, why not have a run for your money, first? I mean, say you're seventeen when you're finally caught – well, gosh, Crab, you'll have *lived* . . .

HAMILTON: Oh, Tich, be your age.

TURNER: I *am* being!

TULLY: Look, it isn't a joke –

TURNER (*passionately*): I *know* it isn't a joke, John, don't be silly. I don't want Crab to make a muck of things, that's all. Parents, Crab – think of your parents. If you're sensible now, they'll probably never hear a thing; the Old Man's very discreet, you know. But what Colonel and Mrs. Crab are going to say if you burst into the sitting-room and announce that you've left in protest at not being allowed to go to bed with Tully of the History Sixth – golly!

TULLY: They'll only send you back, anyway.

HAMILTON: They can't force me.

TULLY: Can't they? As near as dammit they can. They'll try everything. To begin with, your father will roar and chew his moustache, your old Mum will appear at breakfast swollen with a night's sobbing –

TURNER: In her old pink satin jardinière –

TULLY: You won't stand an earthly. They'll use all the unfairest arguments. Your least favourite uncles will be dragged in. There'll be family conferences while you're packed off to the flicks. There'll be every size and colour of emotional blackmail. It'll be wrecking your life just to be fair to me.

HAMILTON: I'm *not* doing it for you, John. Honestly, you seem to think you own me.

TULLY: What have you got to gain by leaving?

TURNER: Well, I should have thought it was pretty obvious – (*roguishly*) eh, Crab?

HAMILTON *shrugs in incomprehension.*

TULLY: Is that it, then?

HAMILTON: No, it isn't.

TURNER (*delighted*): What isn't, what isn't?

TULLY (*rounding on* TURNER): Oh, now, look, we – we shan't be doing any packing for a few minutes.

TURNER (*ruefully indicating the door*): You mean . . .?

HAMILTON: Don't go, Tich.

TULLY (*to* TURNER): I think you'd better – just for a bit.

HAMILTON: Why should he?

TULLY: Are you afraid of being left alone with me, or something?

HAMILTON (*after a pause, unconvincingly*): Of course not.

TULLY (*to* TURNER): Would you mind awfully?

TURNER: OK.OK. I can take a hint.

TULLY: I'll send Tim to fetch you when I'm ready to finish the packing.

TURNER: Righto. Enjoy your scene.

TULLY *makes a gesture of impatience. Exit* TURNER. *There is a pause.*

TULLY: Well?

HAMILTON: Well what?

TULLY: Come off it.

HAMILTON: Come off what?

TULLY: What are you playing at?

HAMILTON: I'm leaving because he sacked you, that's all.

TULLY: But you mustn't. Think of the weight it puts on me.

HAMILTON: Why, is it too much for you?

TULLY: No, of course not, Tim. But there's no sense in making a great thing out of this. You're not a girl, we can't dash off and get married – I mean, can we?

HAMILTON: It's nothing to do with going away together.

TULLY: Then what is it?

HAMILTON: I told you.

Pause.

TULLY (*suddenly*): Well, don't you want to come away with me?

HAMILTON (*caught on the wrong foot*): Why?

TULLY: I only asked if you wanted to.

HAMILTON: Do *you* want it?

TULLY: I'm asking you. (*Silence.*) Look, Tim, give me one good reason for leaving.

HAMILTON: I just don't feel I could stay here on Hallowes' charity, with him being nice and forgiving, as if I'd done something wrong. It would be like admitting we had.

TULLY: I see. (*Pause.*) Well, I can't argue with that. I think you're mad to do it, but if you genuinely feel that way I suppose you must. (*Pause.*) All right, then, let's get to hell out of here, shall we? (*He is suddenly full of tremendous elation.*) We won't go home, we'll break with everything. I'll get my money from the Old Man – I think it's enough for both of us if you'd rather not face him again – I mean, enough to get us somewhere in a train. We'll go where we like: who's to stop us? Look – (*he opens a drawer and produces an aged revolver*) – this works, you know!

HAMILTON (*sadly*): No.

TULLY: It bloody well does! We can feed on crows and rabbits and things –

HAMILTON: Raw?

TULLY: Why not? Jolly nourishing. No, but we'd make fires. And just think, we could sleep in caves – if you don't mind spiders –

HAMILTON: But I do.

TULLY: That's all right. I'll squash them for you. We'd never be found, and we'd be as tough as Sherpas, and I'd grow a beard – you wouldn't – and we'd be absolutely independent and never have to ask anyone for favours – how about it?

HAMILTON (*firmly*): No, John, I couldn't.

Pause.

TULLY (*rather deflated*): Why? It'd be colossal!

HAMILTON: I know it would. I'd love it. But I can't – not yet. Not till I've had a chance to think – away from here, I mean, away from you. – It's all so sudden – everything's changed. You see, I can't remember what it was like before I started going to school. All I remember is trains, and going into school like a long tunnel, and not coming out for two or three months, and then finding myself in the same train going home – only before I knew where I was, it was back heading for the tunnel again. I never realised I could pull the communication cord, or jump out while it was moving. And now, suddenly, I've jumped, or fallen, and the train's going on without me, it's wonderful. But I'm sort of bruised, I can't think, it's as though my head was splitting somehow, or I'd twisted an ankle. And, I mean, really, I want to do without trains for a bit. I want to think, not travel.

Pause.

TULLY: Well, all right, you want to think, that's fair enough; but where will you do your thinking? At home? Is that a good atmosphere for thinking in?

HAMILTON (*reasonably*): It would be all right. I'm used to it.

TULLY: You're not used to it in time of crisis. What about Colonel and Mrs. and the pink jardinière? It would be appalling. You couldn't begin to think.

HAMILTON: Better than here or –

TULLY: Or with me?

HAMILTON: You wouldn't let me think.

TULLY: I couldn't stop you.

HAMILTON: You'd have a darned good try!

TULLY: But why? I should encourage you.

HAMILTON: To think what you think, yes.

TULLY: It's worked pretty well up to now, hasn't it?

HAMILTON: Yes, but . . . Don't you see it's no good just pumping ideas into me? They've got to be *my* ideas before they're worth anything. You've taught me a terrific lot, John, but some things you say I believe in absolutely, and some things I don't, and it all needs sorting out.

TULLY: Well, of course, I've always encouraged you to be independent –

HAMILTON (*with quiet pride*): Yes, and I am being, aren't I?

TULLY: I know, Tim, but you're not strong enough to be independent yet. You'll only make a fool of yourself.

HAMILTON: When am I supposed to be strong enough, then?

TULLY (*evading the issue*): I've got to help you find your way.

HAMILTON (*persisting*): When shall I be strong enough?

TULLY: I don't get this. Is it some line of the Old Man's? Look here, has he told you to break with me?

HAMILTON: Of course he has; but I said I wouldn't.

TULLY: Well, you seem to be doing it pretty effectively.

HAMILTON: Why? Just because I won't run away with you?

TULLY (*hipped*): It's nothing to do with that.

HAMILTON: Then what is it?

TULLY: Just that you're taking this great moral line you can't possibly sustain.

HAMILTON: That'll be my bad luck. I've got to do what I think's right.

TULLY (*fatuously*): So while you do what you think right, I get thrown away like a sucked orange?

HAMILTON (*smiling*): Oh, John, don't be a fool. I don't regret knowing you.

TULLY: I get the impression that you regret it like mad.

HAMILTON (*passionately*): I never will. But surely, it – it was something special. It was right for here, because we were, well, sort of surrounded, like being in a war, and it was the only thing, and it was great. But that's all finished now, and it couldn't be the same outside, could it? It wouldn't mean the same. I expect we'll always be friends, but not like we have been here. Do you see what I mean? (*Pause.*) Do you, John?

TULLY (*slowly*): Yes. I see perfectly.

HAMILTON: I didn't mean to hurt you.

TULLY (*grimly*): It's the only way to make me see anything. – You're absolutely right. The whole point was that it was an emergency measure; and now the state of emergency's over, and the grenadiers can go home. – This is my own medicine, and it tastes bitter.

HAMILTON: Yes, to me too. But you know what they say about medicine.

TULLY: I know what they say. (*Pause.*) I'm just remembering something – something I dreamt last night.

HAMILTON: About medicine?

TULLY: No; about bread. – I dreamt I walked into a huge bakery – you know, with ovens, and racks covered with rolls and buns and cakes and all the pastry you ever saw in your life. Yes, that was it, and – and you were on duty there, in a white apron and a big silly white hat like a chef. I suppose you were the baker's boy.

Anyway, there was no-one else; just this gentle roaring of the ovens, and a haze of flour, and the smell of new bread; it was gorgeous. So I walked up and down, looking at all the cakes and things. There were two enormous long tables right down the middle of the bakery, and lots of elaborate bits of pastry laid out on them, as if it was an exhibition or something, sort of show-pieces. Pies like cathedrals, loaves like wheatsheaves – you know. Yes, it must have been an exhibition, I remember now, because there was a notice outside which said: THIS WAY TO THE SHOWBREAD.

Anyway, I don't know why, but I got up on one of the long tables and started doing place-kicks with these strange-shaped loaves and things that were laid out – trying to land them in an open furnace. You just stood there, and you didn't say a thing, but when I looked at you there were tears streaming down your face. I remember feeling sorry about that, but I was so determined to prove that I could get all these things into the fire, and they were going in so neatly, and burning like fury.

And then . . . my God, yes, I saw you were holding a loaf in your hands – a small ordinary loaf – but in a way it was surprising, because, you know, it was the only one in the place that was just shaped like a loaf and nothing more, just a little white loaf – and it seemed incredible. And you were holding it as if you didn't want me to touch it. But I jumped down from the table and snatched it from you, and chucked it into the fire.

And suddenly I felt cold all over, and I felt I'd done something terrible, so I ran to the fire, and stretched my arm right into the middle to try and pull your heart out . . . I – I mean the loaf. It was there, but not burning, just lying there. And I closed my fingers round it, and as soon as I did that it burst into flames, and then I couldn't move, and I couldn't budge it an inch. Oh, God, I tugged and tugged, and it only burnt faster, and I saw my arm was burning too, and turning to ash, and dropping away in flakes. It didn't hurt, I couldn't feel a thing – but suddenly I gave up. I let go of the little loaf, and at once it stopped burning – just like that – it stopped. And I took my arm out of the fire, and it looked awful, it was so awful I shut my eyes –

And then I woke up, and my arm had gone to sleep because you were lying on it.

Pause.

HAMILTON: I'm sorry.

TULLY: It's all right. I asked for it.

HAMILTON: Thanks awfully for everything.

TULLY (*with a gesture of dismissal*): Oh . . .

Pause. Then, with a rueful defensive brightness:
    Let me know if you change your mind.

HAMILTON (*anything to cheer him*): Yes, of course.

TULLY: But you won't.

Pause.

HAMILTON: Well, goodbye.

He holds out his hand to TULLY. TULLY, astonished, hesitates for a moment, then shakes it solemnly.

TULLY: Goodbye, Tim.

Pause.

HAMILTON: Goodbye.

He turns and goes out quickly without looking round again. TULLY is left dazed. He moves towards the door, but instead of opening it, stands for some moments leaning his forehead against it. Suddenly someone knocks quietly on the door from outside. TULLY starts back. A hope leaps on him.

TULLY: Who is it?

TURNER (*entering*): Only me.

They turn sadly back into the room to continue packing, and . . .

The curtain comes down.

LIES ABOUT VIETNAM

C.P. TAYLOR was born in Glasgow in 1929 but lived in Northumberland for the last twenty years of his life. He wrote over fifty plays for the theatre and television, many of them first performed at the Traverse Theatre, Edinburgh. These include *Bread and Butter* (1966), *The Black and White Minstrels* (1972; subsequently at Hampstead Theatre), *Schippel* (1974; subsequently at the Open Space, London; then retitled *The Plumber's Progress* and starring Sir Harry Secombe, at the Prince of Wales, 1975), *Walter* and *Some Enchanted Evening* (both 1977). *Bandits* was staged by the Royal Shakespeare Company at the Warehouse, London, in 1977. He was closely associated with a community theatre group in Newcastle, Live Theatre Company, for which he wrote, among others, *And A Nightingale Sang . . .* (1977) which was subsequently seen at the Queen's Theatre, London (1979) and on tour. He wrote a great deal for children and young people in the North East, with plays such as *Operation Elvis* (1978), *The Magic Island* (1979) and *Happy Lies* (1981). *Good* was first performed at the RSC Warehouse, London in September 1981. Cecil Taylor died in December 1981.

Lies About Vietnam was first presented at the Traverse Theatre Club, Edinburgh as part of a double bill, alongside *Truth About Sarajevo*, also by C.P. TAYLOR, on 26 May 1969, with the following cast:

CYRIL *a professional protestor, aged 42*	Jonathan Holt
TOM *ex-American airforce officer, aged 24*	William Hoyland
GRAHAM *businessman, old drill sergeant, mid fifties*	Tony Haygarth

Directed by Alan Dosser

Cecil Taylor: A Personal Introduction

I have already written something about *Lies About Vietnam* in the Introduction to this anthology, and I am going to use this opportunity to record particular memories of C.P. Taylor, who died in 1981. We lived a few miles apart in rural Northumberland and from 1973 until his death he was the most important man in my life.

As Head of the English department of a Newcastle upon Tyne comprehensive school, I was able to invite Cecil to help make a film with Super 8 cameras about the lives of the pupils in and out of school. Together with another local playwright, Tom Hadaway, and a gang of wild young film makers, we blazed away with six cameras for a month (we complained about expenditure cuts in those days too!) In the evenings, I joined with other enthusiasts in helping Cecil with his latest production for the Northumberland Youth Theatre and watched his working methods at close quarters.

He wrote most of his 70 plays in a shed at the bottom of his garden. His house was full of children, animals and the constant telephone. In his shed he would blast away at the typewriter, which he battered to destruction. He tried to write at white heat, knowing that he would edit down or discard most of what he wrote. He would always reckon to work through 10 drafts of any project. Producing scripts did not seem to be a problem to him, but shaping and structuring scripts certainly was. He needed to work on drafts of his plays with actors and a director whom he trusted. He shaped his final drafts around the experience of the rehearsal room. In the case of his two *Walter* plays for the Traverse Theatre in Edinburgh, he astounded the company after the first read-through by withdrawing the first of the two plays completely. He told them to get on rehearsing the second play and returned two days later with an entirely new script. His eccentric work method, coupled with his inability to file his various drafts in any sort of order, make the job of producer or publisher especially difficult. His great play *Good*, which was also his last completed masterpiece, was the product of many years and countless drafts, the earliest of which make his indebtedness to the Faust legend far more obvious than is apparent from the published script. The accepted text of *Good* owes a great deal to the hard work of Howard Davies and the Royal Shakespeare Company actors, but whether that text offers the best possible version of the play is open to question since it was prepared for a particular group of actors in a particular, and highly successful, production. As C.P. Taylor's worldwide reputation grows, as it must, researchers will find a wealth of brilliant, unseen and unperformed material in the Taylor archives.

He regarded my own decision to give up teaching and start a career as a playwright openmindedly (I hadn't written a single play at that point), and in spite of his own tremendous workload, he adopted me as his student (as he did with many other aspiring playwrights) and tore my early efforts to shreds. He would take thirty pages of script and mangle the tidy manuscript with his uncoordinated hands for about a minute and a half, and then claim to have read the play. He was as merciless with scripts as he was with directors and producers, most of whom he regarded as fools and idiots. I have heard the reputations of most of the leading British directors reduced to rubble as I drove him to rehearsals at the Traverse, or plotted out the latest projects of the Northern Playwrights' Society, which we founded together. He resented the constant rejection of his plays by London theatres and towards the end of his life turned to television to support his children from two marriages.

The TV detective *Bulman*, now the subject of a successful series, was partly one of his creations. Bulman is just Cecil dressing up. The same trick is played throughout his scripts, whether it's Cecil as the Glasgow comedian *Walter*, or twice in *Good*, as Halder and Maurice (Faust and Mephistopheles), or, more obviously, as Cyril in *Lies About Vietnam*.

Taylor was keenly political, believing at the outset of his career that writing was an important catalyst in social change. Experience forced him to revise his attitude, but even in the earliest plays (as can be seen in the following pages) he knew that home base for a playwright involved creating credible, human characters and setting them in a convincing, dramatic context. The awareness that 'the message' is not everything, and that subtle characterisation is essential, ensures that his plays are durable.

His death was sudden and unexpected. He returned, exhausted, from the RSC's production of *Good* in London, was hospitalised and died overnight. *The Guardian* newspaper billed his new play as 'Goodbye C.P. Taylor'. A savagely funny and prophetic mishap, as it turned out.

Michael Wilcox

REDIFFUSION TELEVISION Limited
INTERNAL MEMO

To ....Head of Scripted Series........   .... 30th June, ...1967

From .....Head of Programme Clearance Tel. Ext. 243 ·   Your Ref. ....

Subject ..HALF HOUR STORY:......"Lies About Vietnam"...... Our Ref. ....
                 by Cecil P. Taylor

         This is obviously a difficult script on two grounds,
political and the personal theme. I think it can be done
subject to the following points being dealt with:

         There should be some warning to viewers of the homosexual
theme so that the play can be avoided and no-one is misled into
viewing by expectations of something else. Probably the only
way of doing this, and certainly it is the easist, is with a
suitable billing. Something like e.g. "A delicate relationship
of Cyril and Tom is nearly upset by the intrusion of Frank"
should do the trick.

         The playing must be very discreet; as the men's situation
is so clearly stated, there should be no touches of business in
the production to emphasize it since any such would inevitably be
regarded as tasteless.

         This having been said and being slotted only in adult time,
all that remains is a need for some detailed cleaning up.

         Even allowing for Tom's "americanisms" I think there are
far more "bloodies" and "Gods" than are legitimately required
for characterization purposes. These should, therefore, be
well pruned.

Page 11 CYRIL: "Tell me love......And I don't want any shit...
                 with a load of shit...."

         This word must be changed. I think the word "crap" only
has been used on television. Associated with the nails and
crucifix image, I think we should be even more careful not to
cause offence by using words such as "nonsense" "rubbish" "dirt"
etc.

ACT ONE

*A room in a third class hotel in a north
east town. Mid-afternoon.*
   CYRIL *and* TOM, *both in pyjamas
and dressing-gowns, are sitting on the
bed, working their way through a chicken
and drinking cheap Spanish wine out of
the hotel tumbler.*
   TOM *has stopped in the act of gnawing
his chicken leg and is staring at it
guiltily.*
   CYRIL *is forty-three. He has the
cultivated good looks of an actor, which
in fact he is – or rather a member of a
branch of that profession – a professional
politician.*
   TOM *is twenty-four and looks eighteen.
He has beautiful, long golden hair, a
tanned body and radiates boyish – or
girlish – innocence. He speaks with a soft
educated American accent. He is a
regular subscriber to* The Greenwich
Village Voice.

CYRIL: You've *bought* the chicken now,
love . . . And the wine . . . The poor,
bloody starving Indians aren't going to
be any the fatter for you throwing it out
of the window! (*Pulling at a wing*) In
any case, I don't mind your
inconsistency . . . It makes me feel
you're real.

The 'phone rings. TOM *watches*
CYRIL *for him to answer it.* CYRIL
gnaws at his chicken, calmly, watching
TOM, *ignoring the 'phone.*

TOM (*looking at the 'phone anxiously*):
We just gonna hold out here, Cyril,
honey? (CYRIL *lifts the 'phone off the
hook.* TOM *tries to enter into this
game of revolt.*) How about us
barricading the door? Push that
wardrobe –

CYRIL: It's that all-American Airforce.
The gracious, soft, air-conditioned
womb. It's ruined you! Worse than a
non-fixated, sexually frustrated mother.

TOM (*throwing himself into the idea of
the barricade*): Wouldn't that be too
much! All the headlines shouting: 'No
War in Vietnam Organisers Besieged
in Hotel Rooms!' That's *too* much,
Cyril! Isn't that too much? Hundreds of
people coming round to the hotel. To
see what it's all about. We go to the

window. 'Friends . . . People . . . We
want to tell you something of the
suffering of the people of Vietnam!'

*He draws at his chicken leg and the
image of the great protest at the same
time.* CYRIL *watches him, his eyes on
the chicken.* TOM *becomes aware of*
CYRIL's *eyes. He stops eating and
looks down, checked in his enthusiasm.*

CYRIL: I've spoiled that chicken for you,
haven't I? That's not fair. You're going
to feel guilty now, every time you have
a square meal. That's wrong. That's
very wrong of me. That wasn't what I
meant to do.

TOM: Hell, Cyril! That's how I *should*
feel! God, man! You've gotta feel
guilty! Shit! That's the only way. To
feel – recognise – your guilt. I saw this
film on television, Cyril. Some state in
India. Kids *crawling* on the ground . . .
Looking for *scraps* of *grain*, man!

CYRIL: Even if – what is it . . . one third?
Two thirds? – of the world wasn't dying
of starvation . . .

TOM's *eyes are on the telephone,
anxious.*

TOM: You don't think they're gonna make
any real trouble . . . call the police
or . . .

CYRIL: The way that chicken has been
reared, Tom . . . There are seeds of
guilt. That's a battery chicken. Did you
know that?

TOM: I got it in the Barbecue . . . Straight
across from the station . . . when we got
in . . .

CYRIL: That's right, love. You got it in
the Barbecue.

TOM: Does that mean it's a battery
chicken?

CYRIL: That's a battery chicken . . .
About . . . I don't know . . . a thousand
chickens all cooped up in so many
square feet of pitch darkness. Not able
to move. Factories for conveying the
minimum amount of grain into the
maximum amount of chicken protein in
the minimum amount of time.

TOM (*looking at the chicken, horrified*):
. . . I know! God, man! I know! This
world! Sometimes it really pulls me
down! Wherever you look. Shit. Shit.

Shit! I mean, sometimes I could just sit there and pull a gun at myself . . . (*His eyes keep going back to the telephone resting on the table*)

CYRIL: You keep staring at that telephone, Tom. Why do you keep staring at that telephone?

TOM: . . . Don't you think we should put it back on its cradle . . . so that we . . . just in case . . . They have anything to say to us . . .

CYRIL: Would you like it back?

TOM: It's just that . . . you know, honey? . . . We don't want to get their backs up and . . .

CYRIL (*replacing it*): There you are. I've put it back, Tom. (*Looking at him*) I don't think you could have pulled a gun on yourself.

TOM: I could! God, I know I could!

CYRIL: The weight of all the world's problems keep pressing on your beautiful, golden head. And sometimes, when they get too much . . .

TOM: They do, Cyril! They do!

CYRIL: You couldn't take a gun to yourself. You're too happy. You enjoy life too much. (TOM *has long gone back to his chicken and wine, eating and drinking with great relish.*) Look at the way you've gone back to that chicken. You've already forgotten that film about India.

TOM (*caught out*): I haven't . . . I . . . I just . . . I just happen to like chicken . . . That's all . . . Sometimes. Shit man! You've *gotta push* those things from your mind . . . Or else you could just . . .

CYRIL: Take a gun to yourself. U.S. Airforce officer takes life. Unable to Bear Guilt for Suffering in Vietnam.

TOM (*looking at 'phone*): You reckon they've given up trying to get us out of here? They're gonna leave us alone?

CYRIL: That manager's a Fred. Fred haircut . . . Fred grey suit . . . Fred eyes popping out of his Fred head when he saw us walking away from the desk, with the room keys. Big panic. Big Fred panic! 'Bloody Pansies! Get those fucking Pansies out of my nice Fred

Hotel! Quick! Pansies out!' . . . Fred's going to try everything in his little Fred book to get us out of here!

TOM: Shit! We have to go and pick a hotel with a fascist bastard manager! Just imagine him, chewing gum, and feeding Jews into the oven! (*Feels* CYRIL *is looking at him strangely.*) Yeah, I know, Cyril . . . Jesus! *I* can talk! Two years doing the same shit job in Vietnam!

CYRIL: Good, all American boy! Did your full service. Obeyed your all-American orders to the last!

TOM: Shit, I would've been shot if I tried to run away! Some of those kids . . . they just got all eaten up, man!

CYRIL: Like Peter and his prisoners . . .

TOM: When I left . . . When my time was up . . . it was just like I had to leave Peter . . . everything was great between us . . .

CYRIL: I'm not interested, love. I am not interested in a single word . . . a single fullstop . . . a single comma . . . that passed between you and Peter!

TOM: This is really great wine. (CYRIL *watches him, sipping the wine.*) You don't like it?

CYRIL: You're so tactful. Aren't you so tactful, Tom?

TOM (*cautiously*): . . . I get lost sometimes when you go in so deep . . . I get lost . . .

CYRIL: So careful, Tom . . . To keep off any possible collision course!

TOM: I don't know what you're talking about . . .

CYRIL: Don't be so bloody stupid. You know what I'm talking about.

TOM: I don't . . . I don't!

CYRIL: I'll ask you a question. If you don't know what I am on about, if you can't handle the minor complexities of a relationship between two people . . . if you get lost, in such a minute gathering. And you have to keep shouting: Where am I? Where am I?

TOM: Cyril. People are *very* complex. You, particularly, are very complex.

CYRIL: If you find yourself absolutely at

sea in such a simple relationship . . . here is the question: how the bloody hell can you set yourself up as an authority in human affairs and presume to dictate to your mighty, complex U.S. all-American Government how they should run the affairs of . . . what is it . . . two hundred million . . . three hundred million people?

TOM: Cyril, that is not a correct analogy . . . that's a debating point. (*As he is speaking, the telephone rings.*)

CYRIL: You are going to stand up on the platform of the City Hall, tonight, in front of all those beautiful, guilty, responsible, aware, informed, lovely people . . . and you are going to tell them what a profound understanding of the situation in Vietnam you have reached after an enforced stay there of two years and how, as a result of this understanding, you have come to the decision that the fighting in Vietnam must be ended, immediately, at all costs . . .

TOM: Shit, man! What's wrong with that? You're going to say the same fucking thing! Shit! (*Looking at 'phone.*)

CYRIL: Here he is! We've been exhibiting him all over the country. This all-American airman. Two years flying air sorties in Vietnam. He has seen with his own eyes the horrors of the actions of his government. He comes to you, the British people, to ask that you demand your Government comes out firmly against this terrible war. We must tell you, however, that we cannot vouch for his understanding of the nature of government or the complexities of world politics. We must point out to you that he is incapable of understanding the forces at play in a simple relationship with just one other person. That person, not even being of the opposite sex . . .

TOM (*smiling at* CYRIL, *grabbing at a chance to divert him*): I guess at a stretch you *could* say 'Not of the opposite sex', honey!

CYRIL (*slowly picking up the 'phone*): Quick! Swerve! Another Collision coming up!

TOM: I like it when you get all kind of worked up into one of those rhetorical

outbursts! Don't know what it is . . . you look just like a kid . . . Real young . . .

CYRIL (*into the 'phone*): Yes . . . Cyril Collins speaking. (*To* TOM) If I took a whip to you, love . . . Would you like that even better? (*into 'phone*) Yes . . . I did get the message . . . Several times . . . Yes . . . Your booking clerk made a mistake . . . He's been telling me that all afternoon . . . *Very* careless of him! Look! I'm sorry you're landed with this problem, I only wish we could help you . . . But . . . you're not serious, are you? Look . . . we have a very important meeting, tonight . . . Even if we did get quickly fixed up elsewhere . . . we haven't the time to waste, packing again and moving . . . I'm sorry . . . I can't help you. Bad luck . . . I hope you'll be able to fix them up somewhere else. Look . . . I'm very sorry . . . I'm in conference just now . . . I haven't got time to hang up talking on the 'phone all afternoon . . . (*Puts down 'phone.*) Fuck you, love! (*To* TOM) Fred, this time. Same old story. Booking Clerk made a mistake . . .

TOM: Cyril . . . I want to give you a very original thought, honey. Maybe there *was* a mistake.

CYRIL (*waiting for the big insight*): Yes . . . Go on . . .

TOM: Maybe there was a mistake . . . a genuine mistake . . .

CYRIL: And . . . (*The 'phone rings again.*)

TOM: A genuine mistake was made. (TOM *waits for* CYRIL *to answer the 'phone. But* CYRIL *sits waiting for* TOM *to elaborate.*) What I'm saying is, Cyril, maybe we were kind of paranoid about the way that manager looked at us.

CYRIL: Paranoid?

TOM *is absolutely aching for* CYRIL *to answer the 'phone.* CYRIL *deliberately ignores it.*

CYRIL: We have delusions of persecution?

TOM: I'm not saying that . . . I mean . . . Maybe . . . Being kind of sensitive . . . We misinterpreted – (*Breaks off. The incessant ringing of the 'phone is getting on his nerves.*)

CYRIL: What about the fucking 'phone? We're misinterpreting that fucking 'phone, screaming at us every minute? What do you mean? Misinterpreting? When he says: Nancy boys, fuck off out of my hotel –

TOM: He didn't say that ... He didn't say anything ...

CYRIL: What he really meant was: 'Do stay and grace my poor hotel with your distinguished, consenting adult fucking presence!' (*In his anger he lifts the 'phone.*) Hullo ... Look ... We're trying to get some work done up here ... I've already told you – A book? I don't know anything about a book. A kind of magazine? Dropped outside our room? What's the title ... *Male Athlete* ... (TOM *is growing more and more uneasy at this conversation.*) I don't know anything about it. I've told you! I know nothing about it! (*Hangs up.*) Did you drop a magazine outside? *Male Athlete*. Sounds like one of your magazines. That was very careless of you, Tom, very careless!

TOM (*beginning to realise what* CYRIL *is doing*): Cyril, honey ... you're not deliberately baiting this manager! Jesus! You're not going out, deliberately to –

CYRIL: They found this magazine. Outside our room.

TOM: It was in my briefcase. The briefcase was all zipped up. It couldn't have ...

CYRIL: I took it out to look through in my bath ... Must have dropped it, myself ...

TOM: You know it kills me when you start going out to bait those people ... I like it nice and quiet and peaceful when we're together ... It used to be so great, Cyril ... So quiet and peaceful ... After the meetings ... and the talking around ... Getting back to our hotel, at night ... I used to find real peace with you, honey ...

CYRIL: It's not a peaceful world. You've got to burn. Burn ... with everybody else, darling ...

TOM: Shit! You don't need to tell me anything about burning ... Every time

I see one of those photographs of kids with napalm burns ... I feel their burns on me. I get my old migraine back ... for days ... you know that?

CYRIL: That's hysteria. Deep seated personality disturbance ... Got fuck all to do with Vietnam, boy! In Vietnam, you went on two air sorties. Two! ... And on both occasions, you dropped warning leaflets ...

TOM: That was just chance! It *could* have been napalm, fragmentaion bombs, rockets ... crop poison ...

CYRIL: But it was leaflets.

TOM: This migraine ... it started from the very first sortie ... and then ... Soon as I was grounded and put into that office job ...

CYRIL: You still kept getting migraine ...

TOM: Just odd attacks ... Most of them when – (*Breaks off.*)

CYRIL: Most of them, when, love?

TOM: I don't remember ... It doesn't matter ...

CYRIL: Most of them when you had those disturbing conversations with Peter, back from his great jungle campaigns against Old Charlie ... That's when you had them, wasn't it? Isn't it? That's why you broke off in mid-sentence, isn't it, Tom? That's why you didn't finish that sentence ...

TOM (*getting a degree more irritated*): You might know the reason for every fucking thing you do! I don't. I just don't! Maybe ... when I'm older ... (CYRIL *doesn't like this.*) ... and I've moved around a bit more ...

CYRIL (*sharply, almost violently*): Tom. Listen to me. Make a note of this. Commit it by heart: I am not remotely, not minutely – not in the *most microscopic degree* – jealous of fucking Peter!

TOM: Cyril, I –

CYRIL: Have you got that? Has that registered?

TOM: I never thought you were jealous of Peter ...

CYRIL: The whole affair bores me to fucking death and beyond! Peter, as described by you, and your futile relationship with him is just as banal, empty and shallow . . . I go to sleep, listening to you going on about it! A prole, illiterate, ignorant, insensitive, sadistic, second-class private from Pittsburgh. Ugly. Overweight. Torso covered with eczema . . .

TOM: He just got intermittent attacks of it. Sometimes his skin would be clear for weeks.

CYRIL: Repulsive – mind and body. Only one thing drawing you together . . .

TOM: That's not right, Cyril! It wasn't like that . . . it wasn't banal! At first . . . we were . . . Some things . . . You just can't put into words . . . you know . . .

CYRIL: Like what? What can't you put into words? Describe them, vaguely . . . (TOM *turns away.*) Draw me a picture of them . . . (TOM *gives it up.*) Fucking Peter even believed in the war he was fighting!

TOM: He didn't believe in it, exactly . . . What happened was . . . sometimes . . . When some of his buddies were killed, by the V.C. . . .

CYRIL: He trooped off into the jungle with his prisoners and carved them up with his G.I. issue chopping knife . . .

TOM: He just did that . . . I don't think . . . more than . . .

CYRIL: Starting, according to your reports, from the pricks, upwards . . .

TOM: That was just once or twice . . . When he got really mad! That was what made me . . . finally break with him . . .

CYRIL: You didn't break with Peter. Peter broke with you. Remember? You haven't the guts to break with anything. That would have been a head-on collision course for you. You would've just kept on, romancing with him, about the beautiful (*'Phone rings again.* CYRIL *lifts it off the cradle without stopping.*) all-American dream of you both going back to Florida, living in a wooden bungalow, on the white beach, backed by an orange-grove . . .

TOM: We talked about other things . . . I haven't told you everything we talked about . . .

CYRIL: You talked about baseball. You hadn't even the remotest interest in baseball . . . But every morning you read up the latest sports news and listened to the radio reports so that you had at least one thing to talk to him about . . . one basis for a dialogue with him other than lust . . . And that went on . . . for how long? Not just for a month or two months . . . But for fourteen fucking months! For fourteen fucking months you put up with that! While he was castrating and mutilating his prisoners, beating up women, frying kids and generally nailing Vietnam on the bloody crucifix of the all-American war industry!

TOM: It wasn't like that . . . We had . . . points of contact . . . He was fascinated with the stars . . . and space and –

CYRIL: And such is the level of your imagination – the insight you have into human behaviour . . . the consummate ability you have in coping with human relations that you actually believed that I was *jealous* of such an empty, shallow, futile, adolescent relationship! All the time, swerving like fucking mad, whenever the subject of Peter came up, accidentally . . . Is that an insight for you, now? Have I spelled it out clearly enough for you? Have you now got a clear, sharp picture of yourself, as seen from outside . . . You think that might help you to grow up that little bit?

TOM: I'm sorry . . . Yes . . . It could be . . . Maybe I . . . not that you were kind of jealous . . . exactly . . . Just that . . . You didn't want to talk about it . . .

CYRIL: Now, that's a different story! That's bang on target, now! You couldn't be more right! I do not want to talk about it. I'd rather talk about how many tons of tarmac go to make the A1 from London to Edinburgh or the number of sperm in an average male load. Peter is just below the level of interest of such topics as those!

TOM: What was so bad about him breaking with me . . . was not knowing why he did it . . . When you lose somebody and you know why . . . God, man! That's hell enough . . . But to lose somebody and not know why . . . Even if he'd stopped speaking to me . . . But he kept on speaking right up till the day I went back home . . . But just word speaking . . . You know . . . Now I've found out he'd taken up with somebody else . . . But God, man! Not to know! That was when I took a gun to myself . . . It got so bad . . . He'd speak to me . . . But it was impossible to ask him . . .

CYRIL: Questions, love. Questions. What happened when you took the gun to yourself? Did you miss? Did you run out of bullets? Did you develop hysterical paralysis of the trigger finger? (TOM *doesn't answer.*) More questions! Why this hot gospel campaign against the Vietnam war? Why? Why are you here, spreading the bad news about Vietnam, instead of taking your Drama degree at Tulano? (TOM *stares at him. Not taking the question seriously.*) Why, Tom?

TOM: You know why! I've been telling people why for the last two months. Night after night . . .

CYRIL: Tell me, love . . . Quietly . . . softly . . . as a personal statement – not as a public, hand on heart, rhetorical fanfare . . . I don't want any shit about you feeling that you were being crucified along with the people of Vietnam . . . And every day you felt another limb being driven personally into your members . . . The crucifix image is getting too heavy, love . . . With the load of shit we keep piling on to it . . . it's toppling over.

TOM *doesn't know how to answer.* CYRIL *is now in too deep for him. He's lost. But* CYRIL *sits, waiting for some reply.*

TOM: *You* know why we're against that war . . . You talk about it every night. You tell hundreds of people about the Passion of Vietnam. That's your words. The Passion of Vietnam.

CYRIL: I've never been in Vietnam. I've only met two Vietnamese in my life – those two Buddhist monks you arranged to come over for the Albert Hall show. I didn't like them. They were too aggressively non-aggressive. They gave me a big pain in the arse. No . . . Tell me, love . . . What is it, that drives you to campaign against this war. Tell me, Tom. (TOM *turns away. Sure he is being teased. And sulking just a little.*) Is it the burns? You feel the burns?

TOM: You know I get this migraine . . .

CYRIL: All the way from Vietnam?

TOM: You know fucking well why . . . You know yourself, why you get so burned up about this. You're just projecting now . . . Just giving out a load of shit . . .

CYRIL: I don't want to die, Tom . . . I like it here . . . I don't want you to die . . . that bloody war your mates have started out there, is a threat to my continued existence . . . I'm not prepared to go out there and put bandages on the wounded . . . And risk getting some fucking disease . . . And put up with all that fucking heat and rain and discomfort . . . (*As he is talking there is a knock at the door.*) The kids dying of burns, and the blown up villages, and the tortured V.C. . . . it's just pictures in the papers or the telly to me . . . Or articles in the papers . . . Or stories in the pamphlets we hand out . . . That's real to me. That's the front line between the fucking East and West, boy . . . If they can make a deal – there's a good chance of my dying some kind of natural death . . . somewhere in my sixties or seventies . . . I like it here. (*The knocking is now insistent.*) If they don't make that deal . . . I'll be obliterated before I reach fifty . . . if I'm lucky . . . if my luck's out, I could have to hang on for a slow, lingering, stinking, repulsive death that could take anything up to a year . . . two years . . . Ugliness, misery, stink and shit all round me! That's my stake in your fucking war, love! (*The knocking is louder.*)

TOM: Shouldn't we answer that door?

VOICE (*outside*): Frank Graham here. Could I please have a word with you!

CYRIL (*to* GRAHAM): Just a minute, please . . . We're in the middle of some calculations . . .

GRAHAM: This won't take long . . .

CYRIL: Who did you say was there?

GRAHAM: I've been trying to get you on the 'phone.

CYRIL: Just one minute, please. Just finishing this calculation . . . (*To* TOM, *quietly:*) That photograph you have . . . Of your all-American mother and sisters . . . Give me it.

TOM: Don't go out of your way to –

CYRIL: Give me that photograph, will you?

TOM *produces a photograph from his wallet.*

CYRIL: Fine . . . Great . . . Got your Airforce Book, handy . . .

TOM: It's in my case . . . Look.

CYRIL: Get it out.

He goes into his own case, brings out some campaign photographs, burned children, a flamethrower, rockets, effects of a napalm raid.

GRAHAM (*knocking*): Are you going to be much longer, there?

CYRIL (*going to door*): Coming, Mr Graham . . . Coming.

He turns the handle and admits GRAHAM. FRANK GRAHAM bursts into the room, raging but in some control of the violence the two homosexuals rouse in him. Everything he sees confirms his original diagnosis of 'queers'. The black nylon pyjamas of the older man, TOM's shortie dressing-gown and golden hair, the disturbed bed and general untidyness of the room. He sniffs and detects perfume. Stares at CYRIL and thinks he sees a trace of lipstick.
FRANK is in his fifties, short, red-faced, wiry. Everything CYRIL stands for, FRANK recognises immediately, he hates with all his soul and all his might, as CYRIL hates everything FRANK stands for.
He's been messed around enough now, by those two queers. He's standing no more nonsense. At the same time, there is a way of doing those things – and there is a way of not doing them – FRANK can handle these characters alright.

GRAHAM: Now, look here! We don't want any unpleasantness. Just pack your bags and vacate the room. Come on, now!

CYRIL stares, waiting for him to elaborate . . . he is very much in control of the situation.

CYRIL: Mr Graham! You haven't come up all those stairs just to tell us that, again?

GRAHAM: Come on. I'm trying to play fair with you . . . you play fair with me . . .

CYRIL: You've already delivered that message . . . oh . . . at least half-a-dozen times on the 'phone. Mr Graham . . . You've obviously got problems, Mr Graham. Tell us about them. But briefly as you can, please. We've still a lot of work to get through before our meeting, tonight.

GRAHAM: Look, friend . . . The party that booked this room weeks ago, is expected any minute now . . .

TOM (*trying to be nice and reasonable and counter CYRIL's baiting*): You see, Mr Graham, we have this big meeting on tonight and to prepare for it we –

CYRIL: Tom, Mr Graham's not interested in our problems. He has his own . . .

GRAHAM: Too true I have!

CYRIL: He is responsible for the efficient running of this hotel . . . And he has found a key member of his staff absolutely incompetent.

GRAHAM: The maid is waiting outside, to get the room tidied up.

CYRIL: As the manager of the hotel, he has the responsibility of resolving what would seem to be an unresolvable problem.

GRAHAM: I've solved it alright, friend . . . And I'm not the manager of the hotel.

CYRIL: Yes. I would say we're pretty well on the way to resolving it, together, Mr Graham. You say, you're not the manager?

GRAHAM: I have no official position here. I'm a personal friend of Mrs Meadows – the proprietress and manageress of the hotel. That's all you need to know.

TOM (*nicely*): You acting as a kind of representative, Mr Graham, is that it? Of Mrs Meadows . . .?

GRAHAM: I keep a friendly eye on Mrs Meadow's interests.

TOM (*meaning it*): That's nice, Mr Graham.

CYRIL: You have shares in the hotel?

GRAHAM: There is such a thing, friend, as helping people just for the satisfaction of helping them . . . not for what's in it for you.

TOM: I believe that very much, Mr Graham. I do . . . I think that just about rates as the ultimate in happiness . . . Helping people . . . unselfishly . . . just out of love.

CYRIL (*going out to shatter the image TOM is projecting*): Oh, that magazine, Mr Graham . . . that you found in the hall . . .

GRAHAM (*producing it as the ultimate evidence that is going to drive the two from the hotel*): This . . .

CYRIL: That's it. It turned out, my friend dropped it. On his way to the bathroom.

GRAHAM (*handing it to* TOM, *as if it was diseased*): Then you'd better take it back, hadn't you . . . And you want to be careful, friend! Dropping filth like that in public places.

TOM (*embarrassed, flushing*): Mr Graham . . . I hope you haven't got the wrong impression about that book . . . It just happened . . .

GRAHAM: I'm an old army man, son. I know all about those kinds of book! I've had the type of character that goes for filth like that through my hands time out of number . . . Soft, that's the whole problem. Lack of self-control. No control over themselves.

CYRIL: I couldn't understand what my friend was doing with a magazine like that . . .

GRAHAM: I know all about those books, alright. And the characters that carry them about.

CYRIL: You see, what happened was, Mr Graham . . . My friend is an athlete . . .

GRAHAM: The damage books like that do!

TOM: A sprinter, Mr Graham. I did some high jumping . . . But I wouldn't rate myself a jumper.

GRAHAM: You look into one of those books . . . See the filthy photographs

. . . And the obscene adverts . . . And you say to yourself 'Other people are doing those things. Why shouldn't I?'

TOM (*seizing on a jumping off ground for dialectics*): Yes, Mr Graham . . . That's the kind of key question, isn't it? Now we've thrown God onto the scrapheap along with all those other obsolete concepts . . . like Courage . . . Patriotism . . . Respect . . .

GRAHAM: That's exactly what I'm talking about, son. You throw all those things out that went to make man different from wild animals and what are you left with? (*Turning on* CYRIL:) A soft, flabby, spineless, jellyfish.

TOM: What I was going to say, Mr Graham, was . . . if you throw all those things away . . . or rather now that history has proved them kind of empty concepts . . . then that makes it very difficult to answer your key question, 'Why shouldn't I?'

CYRIL: We came up from Liverpool, today. We stopped at a bookstall on the way to the station . . . My friend, being an athlete, saw this magazine on the stall –

GRAHAM: That's another thing. I'd bloody well make sure the people that sold that kind of filth got a minimum of a year's imprisonment without the option. It doesn't matter how much you fine the bastards. They just stick it on to the price of their filthy books! (*Taking the magazine for a moment:*) Look at that! (*Flicks through the pages.*) Twenty pages . . . And seven and a tanner! And the books and photographs they advertise inside! Two and three guineas a set of photographs! They're making a bloody fortune!

CYRIL (*continued*): My friend sees this magazine, *Athletic Male*. He immediately buys it . . . he hasn't had time to examine it . . .

TOM: Yeah . . . That was one hell of a rush to get that train, wasn't it, hone-. . . Cyril?

GRAHAM: What are you trying to prove, friend? I've told you time out of number. The room's been previously booked.

CYRIL: He immediately identifies it with his favourite sport. Hands over his money . . . and only when he is sitting back in his carriage does he realise that he has bought a pornographic magazine.

GRAHAM: What are you trying to prove?

CYRIL *looks at him for a moment . . . playing him, like a fish . . . which way is he going to turn him, now?*

CYRIL: I think we should be honest with one another, Mr Graham. Come on, now . . . What is running at the back of your mind . . . the big problem, weighing on you, Mr Graham . . . is that somehow or other . . . we are not desirable guests . . . That's it, isn't it?

GRAHAM: I'm not interested in what you are, friend. The room has been previously booked.

CYRIL: You find this book outside our room and, naturally, you jump to the conclusion that we are – to call a spade a spade, Mr Graham – homosexuals.

GRAHAM: Look, friend . . . I'm an old army man . . . I wasn't born bloody yesterday. When a middle-aged man – if you want to start calling spades spades, friend – comes into a hotel with a young lad, half his age, with long blonde hair like a girl . . .

CYRIL: Women like long blonde hair in a man . . . Did that not occur to you, Mr Graham . . . He has his hair in that style to please his wife.

GRAHAM: Let me finish, will you! You characters never let anybody have their say out! You walk upstairs into your bedroom, in the middle of the afternoon . . . Draw the curtains . . . Go into the bathroom together . . . We find this book in the hall . . . We're running a hotel, friend . . . A business . . . You think that kind of thing's going to encourage guests? Now, come on. We don't want any unpleasantness. Just pack your bags and –

CYRIL (*to* TOM): Did you hear all that, Tom? You heard all Mr Graham said there, quite clearly?

TOM: Well . . . I guess . . . It could look kind of like –

GRAHAM: Come on, friend! The maid's waiting –

CYRIL: Take it easy, Mr Graham! Steady, now . . . You want to watch what you're saying. You could be making a very big mistake.

GRAHAM *is uneasy at the threat . . . he begins to run through the evidence in his mind . . . and, as if* CYRIL *is reading his thoughts,* CYRIL *reinterprets the meaning of all this evidence.*

I've already explained the book, I realise there is a trend these complicated days we're living in, to search out the most complex explanation for a simple action. Your interpretation of us getting into pyjamas and drawing the curtains is a perfect example of this. Mr Graham . . . In fact, the true explanation is absolutely simple . . . We have been travelling all the previous night . . . and all of this morning. We were quite simply utterly exhausted and in desperate need of a hot bath and then some sleep, to prepare us for a very hard conference tonight.

FRANK *is not convinced. But at the same time he begins to waver a fraction.*

GRAHAM: I've seen this kind of thing time and time again in the army. Don't give me any –

TOM: Did you see much fighting in the army, Mr Graham?

GRAHAM (*drawing himself up*): I was the heart of the army. I *made* soldiers. Drill Instructor. Tell you this, son . . . If either of you had spent six weeks under my instruction, you wouldn't be where you are today! Every lad that passed through my hands I can guarantee you, came out firm, physically and morally.

TOM (*putting it up as a point to be considered by* GRAHAM. *Possibly to move him towards a more progressive stance*): Have you ever considered, Mr Graham, that some of the greatest inhumanities have been initiated by what you might call the most morally firm characters?

GRAHAM *looks at him.*

CYRIL: What are you trying to establish, Tom?

GRAHAM: What do you mean, friend?

TOM: Cromwell, for example . . .

GRAHAM: Cromwell?

TOM: Hitler, then . . . To come nearer our time . . .

GRAHAM: Now there you are then! If Hitler wasn't a queer, he was halfway on the road . . . And his bloody henchmen. Don't tell me about Hitler, son . . . I know all about Hitler. Now . . . Do us a favour . . . Get your things packed.

CYRIL: Mr Graham. I thought we'd established this long ago. Leaving the hotel, or even changing rooms at this late hour, when we have still so much to do is out of the question, Mr Graham. You have no official position in the hotel, so we'll just forget all about your mistaken accusation of us being homosexuals . . . The best thing for you to do now, Mr Graham is to leave us to get on –

GRAHAM: Look, friend. I'm an old soldier . . . And a businessman. That's one of the tools of my job – summing up people, rightly . . .

TOM: Oh, you're in business, now, Mr Graham. I think there's a lot of mistaken prejudice against businessmen . . . You know? People don't consider that while we have this kind of society that is based on business, somebody has to do the dirty work of that society . . .

CYRIL: What in the name of God, Tom, do you mean by that inane remark?

GRAHAM: He's absolutely right. Business is the backbone of the country.

TOM (to CYRIL): I mean . . . Business people get all the bricks thrown at them . . . Whatever goes wrong in this society . . . they get the bricks. My father's in business, back home, Mr Graham. He has a leathercraft store. What kind of business are you in, Mr Graham?

GRAHAM (beginning to warm to the younger man. In fact he has been, despite himself, charmed by his charming manner all along. He finds he has some very sound ideas. He looks at him and the other man, becoming a little less sure yet of his initial diagnosis): I'm in the manufacturing . . . I make toys.

TOM: That's nice business. That's a real, social kind of business, isn't it? Making toys.

GRAHAM (warming still more): I get a lot of satisfaction out of it . . . Lot of satisfaction out of it . . . Thinking of the pleasure I'm giving all those kids . . .

TOM: Oh . . . It's a real, beautiful job, Mr Graham.

GRAHAM: You know what started me off in it, son? I was in the joinery trade before that . . . My grandchildren . . . They started me off on the whole thing.

TOM: You've got grandchildren . . . That's nice . . .

GRAHAM: Used to keep buying them toys . . . Some of them not cheap, either . . . Two or three quid, some of them. We'd go back to their house a week or so later – and they'd be broken . . . Not the kids' fault . . . I mean . . . A toy's got to be made to stand the rough handling kids give them . . . No . . . Just the shoddy way they'd been made.

TOM: So you thought you'd go and try to give the kids a square deal.

GRAHAM: Those were my exact words, son! I got a few good lads together . . . An old church hall . . . And I've never looked back . . . Never looked back, to this day! Got twenty men working for me . . . My stuff's in the best shops all over the country . . . Get written-up in the papers . . .

TOM: It's real socially useful business, Mr Graham.

GRAHAM: Don't get me wrong, son . . . I don't make any fortunes out of it . . . But it pays its way . . . Growing a bit, every year . . .

CYRIL (producing TOM's photograph of his mother and sisters): I'm afraid my two children, Mr Graham, are a bit past the toy age . . . Or I might have given you an order . . . (TOM passes the photograph to GRAHAM. GRAHAM studies it . . . he begins to move still further from his initial suspicion.) My friend, now, should be a likely customer for you . . . He has a five year old. (to TOM:) Tom . . . Where's that photograph of your boy?

TOM (*confused. Unhappy at the deception*): ... I haven't ... I don't know, Cyril ... I don't think ...

GRAHAM (*returning the photograph to* CYRIL): Nice girls ... (*To* TOM:) You just got the one?

TOM: Yes ... Yes ...

GRAHAM: Time enough, eh?

CYRIL (*taking up* TOM's *wallet on the table*): I'm sure I saw a photograph in your wallet ... (*Bringing out* TOM's *U.S.A.F book.*) Inside your airforce book ... (*Looking:*) No ... (*Showing* GRAHAM *the photograph of* TOM *in the book:*) Vicious looking photograph that, isn't it?

GRAHAM (*looking*): Oh ... You're an air force man.

CYRIL: Been in Vietnam most of his service ... Very tough character, Mr Graham ... Hundred sorties man, Tom! Destroyed goodness knows how many Vietcong villages ... It's only a couple of days, since he was walking the streets of Saigon!

GRAHAM: I've seen some of the war there on television ... Looks bloody hell out there!

TOM: It's pretty horrible, Mr Graham.

CYRIL: Keep this strictly to yourself, Mr Graham ... But Captain Blake is on a special mission that could bring badly needed business into this country. A new air-to-ground, fragmentation missile ...

GRAHAM (*looking toward the photographs* CYRIL *has deliberately laid out for him*): Yes ... I was wondering what these photographs were doing, there ...

CYRIL: With a bit of luck, I'm hoping to persuade him to place an order for those missiles with the firm I work for ... I'm a technical, weapons consultant ... An old army man, like yourself ... Commandos, during the war ...

TOM: A high ranker, Mr Graham ... A colonel ...

CYRIL: Lieutenant Colonel ... War finished before I could reach a full one ...

GRAHAM *has now completely swung* over. He moves automatically back into his N.C.C./C.C. role ... The whole gestalt is changed. The scent is obviously now high class shaving lotion. The pyjamas and dressing-gown the bourgeois tastes of the officer class. The hairstyle of TOM the result of having no time for a haircut in between sorties ... etc ... etc ...

GRAHAM: I don't know all the ins and outs of this business, sir ... But it seems to me, we've been involved in too many of those kind of wars in the past ... we want to keep out of this war, if we can.

CYRIL: You're absolutely right! I couldn't agree more! I certainly don't think we should get involved to the extent of actually fighting with the Americans. But at the same time, Mr Graham, we should try to realise what the Americans are trying to do out there ... Desperately struggling to contain Communism. And we should back them in every possible way, short of actually sending our own boys to fight.

GRAHAM: Oh, I'm with you there, sir. I'm definitely with you there.

CYRIL: I don't think that some of the evil of Communism is generally recognised, Mr Graham ... But to hark back to what you were worried about, earlier ... homosexuality ...

GRAHAM: I'm very sorry about that, sir ... I don't know what –

CYRIL: Forget all about your mistake, Mr Graham ... My own position on homosexuality is neutral ... I think if the adults do keep it between themselves in the spirit of this bill ... Good and well ... So long as they are legally prevented from corrupting the youth.

GRAHAM: That's the whole problem, sir ... The way they spread this moral poison. They get hold of young, innocent lads ... Before they've had a chance to find out what life is about ... and inject them with their own poison! That's what eats me up about the whole business, sir!

CYRIL: To get back to what I was saying, Mr Graham, it's not generally known, but one of the nastier elements of this communist conspiracy to take over the world is the way it exploits such sexual deviations as homosexuality . . . as a means of injecting moral decay into the countries they want to undermine. A kind of psychological germ warfare.

GRAHAM: Yes . . . I've read something about that, sir. Look what's happening on our own doorstep! This bill they've got before Parliament to let them carry on just as they want . . . We all know who's organised that, eh, sir?

CYRIL: What it all adds up to, Mr Graham, is that the Americans, in taking it upon themselves to hold the dyke against an enemy that resorts to filthy tactics like that, are fighting in the name of all of us right thinking people and no right thinking person can or should opt out of supporting them in this struggle short, as I say, of actually taking up arms, themselves. Yes . . . I know you're going to bring up the question of *American* atrocities. (GRAHAM *wasn't going to bring up any such thing.*) Children being roasted alive by napalm. Innocent civilians killed and maimed by fragmentation bombs . . . women raped and mutilated . . . crops that have cost the Vietnamese a lifetime of work destroyed by poisons . . . Of course, these things are happening . . . civilians being killed . . . But that is war, Sergeant . . . You *were* a Sergeant, in the war, weren't you?

GRAHAM: That's right, sir. Drill-Sergeant, sir.

CYRIL: And expressed as a percentage of the Vietcong killed, the civilian deaths are very small . . . That's true, isn't it, Tom?

TOM (*torn between pleasing* CYRIL *by joining in this baiting of* GRAHAM *and his desire to be sincere and truthful with* GRAHAM): It's pretty considerable . . . I haven't got exact figures . . . But the number of innocent . . . women . . . and kids, Cyril . . . that just happen to get between us and the V.C. are –

CYRIL: Exactly. That's the whole point, Tom. That's Vietcong technique . . . Operating from peaceful villages, deliberately, endangering the lives of innocent civilians . . .

TOM: Yeah . . . Well . . . That does happen from –

CYRIL: Advance warning is sent out before a raid . . . The Vietcong know bloody well when they're coming . . . But they deliberately use those innocent people as one of their techniques of war . . . Holding them at gunpoint . . . I'll ask you, Sergeant, as an old army man, what kind of soldier is it, who fires behind a living barricade of innocent civilians?

GRAHAM: Bloody hell, sir! Even the Nazis didn't go so low as that! I didn't know they went in for that kind of thing, sir!

CYRIL: That's just a fraction of the story, Mr Graham . . . Some of the things they do . . . I just couldn't even talk about!

GRAHAM: That's the whole trouble, sir, isn't it? You watch the telly and you read the papers and you get ideas about the situation in Vietnam and Rhodesia . . . and that . . . But you never know what's really going on there, unless you go out and see for yourself what's happening on the spot . . .

CYRIL: You see . . . (*He is now coming to his goal . . . he's turned* GRAHAM *and is now going to establish to* TOM *and himself how deep* GRAHAM's *reaction goes.*) You're dealing with a very backward civilisation . . . Intelligence is not one of the strong points of the element that are attracted to ideas like Communism. It takes a long time for the message that they can't possibly win to get through to them. It's got to be hammered in. Like we hammered it into the Japs at Hiroshima and Nagasaki . . . (*Going to his campaigning charts:*) That's the idea of weapons like this. You're an old army man, Sergeant . . . We can rely on your discretion to keep those pictures to yourself . . .

GRAHAM: Absolutely, sir! Absolutely!

CYRIL: This is the type of rocket we're negotiating about . . . (*Showing him some pictures of burned children, civilians, villages*) Two or three prototypes have been already in operation in Vietnam . . . There's some pictures of the effects. Pretty effective, aren't they, Tom? (TOM *weighs what to say in the balance, he won't be seeing* GRAHAM *after tomorrow, and he's likely to be with* CYRIL *a long time* . . .) Just took three to flatten this whole village, didn't it Tom?

TOM (*forces himself to join in* CYRIL's *baiting*): Yes . . . About three . . . (*Bringing some of his photographs*) That's a picture of the village before we dropped the missiles . . . And that's a series, after the raid.

GRAHAM (*looking*): Not much of that place left, eh, sir?

TOM (*producing some more pictures*): Those are some of the injured we picked up, after the raid. They'd been in the periphery of the village . . . There were no survivors in the target area . . .

GRAHAM (*examining them*): Bit of a state, aren't they, sir?

TOM (*well into enthusiastic American airman role now*): Reckon there wasn't many of old Charlie left, the time we'd finished there! . . . Yes . . . Some kids on the periphery got burned bad . . . Hell, man! It kills you, maiming innocent kids like that! I mean . . . When you go in after it's all over and you see them . . . and hear them screaming . . . and that kind of horrible stink . . . of human beings . . . people . . . burning. But that's Old Charlie! They don't know how to fight clean!

GRAHAM (*shaken by the photographs, but at the same time loyal to his principles*): Yes . . . I know what you're up against . . . (*Hypnotised by the burnt children.*) It's just . . . sometimes . . . you can't help thinking . . . if it was my grandchildren . . . but . . . that's the way God works, isn't it? He works in strange ways . . .

TOM: You believe in God, Mr Graham?

CYRIL (*bored with the game, now time he got rid of* GRAHAM. *Dismissing him*): I wish we had time to go on with this interesting chat, Mr Graham . . . but time presses on.

GRAHAM: Sorry, sir! I'm a terrible character for gassing on.

CYRIL: We'll have to get together later . . . After our conference, maybe. And continue our talk . . . It's not every day you meet with somebody who has something to say . . . Maybe when we get back, tonight . . . (*Moving towards the door.*)

GRAHAM: Any time, sir . . . I'll be around here . . . Most of the evening.

TOM: I wish I could believe in God. I wish I really could believe that he existed and you could depend on him . . . Something like that . . . It would be great . . .

GRAHAM: He's there, alright, sir . . . Working for us all the time.

TOM: You reckon he is, Mr Graham?

CYRIL: Mr Graham . . . sorry – (*Pushing him gently to the door.*)

GRAHAM (*stopping in the doorway, to* TOM): Oh, yes. He's there . . . Definitely . . . He's there, sir. What He is . . . is . . . you know . . . people trusting each other . . . You know the kind of thing? Having faith in each other . . . I mean . . . love . . . If you could just get governments speaking to each other just like we're speaking, just now . . . At first, a bit suspicious . . . kind of not trusting each other . . . and then . . . well . . . you know? At last kind of finding God in each other . . .

TOM: Yes . . . I can see it your way . . . Breaking through that barrier of mistrust and hate . . .

CYRIL (*pushing* GRAHAM *out*): We might have a drink together, when we get back . . . Yes?

GRAHAM: Pleasure, sir . . . (*To* TOM:) It was a boy you had, sir, wasn't it?

TOM: Yeah . . . A boy . . . Yeah . . .

GRAHAM *finally goes out.* CYRIL *throws the bed clothes back and falls into bed.* TOM *sits on the easy chair, thinking.* CYRIL *watches him.*)

CYRIL: We learn . . . every day we learn, Tom . . . What have we learned today, love? One: God is Love. That's what He is – Love. Two: That God is to be found in communication with a U.S. Airforce officer, fresh back from his personal Buchenwald in Vietnam, and a rocket manufacturer, about to help him to step up the already mounting death rate there, rather than in communication with a young, blonde,

American homosexual and his professional protesting leftwing boyfriend . . .

TOM *is alienated by his tone which normally would have amused him and struck sparks of further argument from him.*

TOM: See . . . What I was trying to do, Cyril . . . was avoid areas of conflicts . . . I wanted us always to keep inside areas of understanding . . .

CYRIL: It's alright, love. Don't worry about it . . .

TOM: What you were trying to say to me, Cyril . . . was that by avoiding those areas of conflict . . . I was narrowing down our areas of understanding . . . Is that what you meant, Cyril?

CYRIL: Forget about it, love . . . That's you, isn't it? That's you. Sometimes, it irritates, but mostly . . . (*Stretching out a hand to him:*) . . . it's endearing . . . (*As he is speaking, there is a knock on the door.*) God! These people! Won't leave us in peace a fucking minute! (*To the door:*) Yes?

GRAHAM (*outside*): It's me, again. Can I come in, just for a minute . . .

CYRIL (*getting out and sitting on bed*): Yes . . . Yes . . . Come on, Mr Graham.

GRAHAM *enters, carrying a jack-in-the-box. He gives it to* TOM.

GRAHAM: While it was still in my mind . . . my place is just next door . . . I thought I'd bring it up now . . . in case, I missed you . . . For your boy . . . That's the kind of thing we make.

TOM (*moved*): You made it! In your factory . . . Oh . . . It's great! Thanks . . . It really is . . . It's great! Thanks, Mr Graham . . . Thanks.

GRAHAM (*going*): Better let you get on with your work, eh? Well . . . Maybe see you later . . .

TOM: Sure . . . yeah . . . sure . . . Mr Graham . . . Thanks. thank you very much! It really is . . . it's beautiful!

TOM *sits and admires his jack-in-the-box. He opens the lid. The jack-in-the-box jumps up. He is greatly moved by it and by the act of* GRAHAM's *giving him the present.* CYRIL *watches him, cynically, impatient . . . to get him into bed.*)

CYRIL: Let me see it, love . . . Let me see it, Tom . . . (TOM *is engrossed in the toy.*) Yes . . . I'm sure your little lad will love it, won't he, love? (TOM *is still absorbed in the toy, playing with it, fascinated.*) Tom . . . Won't your little lad love it . . . Come on . . . Don't be boring, love. Bring it over here . . . I've always been fascinated by jack-in-the-boxes. (TOM *continues to stare at the box.*) Tom . . . The meeting starts at seven . . . We haven't all that much time left . . . Come on, love . . . (*Holding out his hand.*) Let's look for God, together . . .

TOM *puts the box down, carefully on the table. He stands, looks at it a moment, then slowly comes over to the bed, taking off his dressing-gown.* CYRIL *looks at his face, and then over to the box. The sadness of* TOM *moves him, engulfs him. So that when they finally embrace it is with great sadness.*

Curtain.

BEARCLAW

For Victor

TIMOTHY MASON has spent most of his life working in theatre, first as an actor in his native Minneapolis, and then as a playwright. He has won the National Society of Arts and Letters Award, a playwriting fellowship from the National Endowment for the Arts, the Twin Cities Drama Critics Circle Award, and was nominated for *Newsday*'s Oppenheimer Award. His plays include *In a Northern Landscape*, first produced by the Actors Theatre of Louisville in 1983; *Levitation*, which premiered in New York at the Circle Repertory Company in 1984; *Bearclaw*, initially presented in 1984 by Lucille Lortell and Circle Repertory at the White Barn Theatre in Westport, Connecticut; and *Before I Got My Eye Put Out*, commissioned in 1984 by the South Coast Repertory in Costa Mesa, California. He also wrote seventeen plays for young audiences which were produced by the Minneapolis Children's Theatre Company. Mr. Mason lives and works in New York City.

Bearclaw was first presented by Lucille Lortell and the Circle Repertory Company of New York at the White Barn Theatre, Westport, Connecticut, on 10 August 1984. The cast, in order of appearance, was as follows:

PAUL *22*   Bruce McCarty
CONSTANCE *mid-30s*   Katherine Cortez
PETER *68*   Richard Seff
PETER Jr *mid-30s*   Richard Cottrell

Directed by B. Rodney Marriott
Setting by James Wolk

Bearclaw was subsequently revised and produced in the present version by the Seattle Repertory Company, Seattle, Washington, on 29 March 1985, with the following cast:

PAUL   Donald Mantooth
CONSTANCE   Lori Larsen
PETER   John Eames
PETER Jr.   R. Hamilton Wright

Directed by Kevin Tighe

Bearclaw was originally commissioned by the Actors Theatre of Louisville.

Notes on production: In the stage directions, the transitions between the ten scenes are often indicated by a shift in the colour and/or intensity of the lighting. Thus, an interval of several weeks may transpire without the lights going to black. Alternatively, the director may choose to separate each scene with total darkness. I've seen the play produced effectively both ways. Finally, the director may find advantages in casting a black actress in the role of Constance.

Bearclaw

My father spent many years as a national advocate for the elderly, doing his best to expose what he called 'warehouses for the living dead', and to create decent, humane homes for the aged. (The nursing home in this play is one of the latter.) I think the fact that several of my plays are inhabited by older characters stems from an early exposure to my father's labours.

Bearclaw is a story about what sons receive, or fail to receive, from their fathers. As explicated by Paul, the young American Indian orderly, the bear's claw has the potential either to nurture the bear cub, or to destroy it.

I've always loved the story of the Prodigal Son from the Gospel of Luke. A certain man had two sons, one of whom takes his inheritance and, in squandering it, nearly destroys himself. When he returns to beg his father's forgiveness, the father puts a ring on his finger and a robe on his shoulders and lays on a big feast for the boy. The elder son, who has remained at home, dutiful, obedient and perhaps a little boring, is angry and refuses to attend.

The image of the generous father embracing his wayward son has always moved me. At the same time, I've always felt the older son had a legitimate complaint.

Bearclaw is also about a very personal brand of fascism, one that can be practised in the comfort of one's own home. Perhaps the initial impulse behind any fascistic act is benevolent. The danger arises when one confuses a desire to do good for others with a conviction that one knows what is best for them.

There are no villains in the piece, unless time itself is counted as an enemy. There are only some major failures and some minor triumphs. Perhaps that's the best one can expect, given the odds.

Timothy Mason

Scene One

A nursing home in St Paul, Minnesota.

As the house goes to black, a voice on the public address system: 'Testing, two, three. Good morning. The title of Reverend Wee's sermon this Sunday will be "Life at the Crossroads." Special music will be provided by the St. Paul Cathedral School Boys Choir. Remember now, that's Sunday, 10 a.m. in the chapel, "Life at the Crossroads."'

Morning light. A clean, well-appointed room in a modern nursing home. PAUL *is making up the bed, while* CONSTANCE *goes through closets and drawers, collecting leftover odds and ends.* PAUL *is dressed as an orderly;* CONSTANCE *is dressed as a nurse.*

They work in silence for some time.

PAUL: How can you tell if you've got a hernia?

CONSTANCE: Believe me, you'd know. (*Finding a pair.*) Shoe-trees. You need any?

PAUL: For sneakers?

CONSTANCE *looks at* PAUL's *feet, then drops the shoe-trees into a bag and turns back to the closet.*

Mrs. Swenson. God. Blimping right out on me. She calls, I come, I lift, I put her down on the toilet. I wait. She thinks. She *hums*. She says she's not in the mood. Lift, carry, back to the bed, plunk. Ten minutes later, she calls again.

CONSTANCE: Feel your groin.

PAUL: That's a habit I'm trying to break.

CONSTANCE: Go on. Is there a lump on either side? Is it tender?

PAUL (*feeling*): A little tender. No lumps.

CONSTANCE: You'll be fine.

PAUL: Easy for you to say.

CONSTANCE (*finding a small object at the bottom of a drawer*): Weird ring.

PAUL: Lemme see.

CONSTANCE (*giving it to* PAUL): It's huge.

PAUL: It's an ashtray.

CONSTANCE: An ashtray?

PAUL: I love it.

CONSTANCE: It's yours.

PAUL: I mean it, I love it.

CONSTANCE: Catch you smoking on the floor again, your ass is grass.

PAUL: I know, I know.

They work in silence for a time.

CONSTANCE: Your father was out here again this morning.

PAUL: Right.

CONSTANCE: You found him?

PAUL: I found him.

CONSTANCE: Sprawled out in the lobby when I came on.

PAUL: I took care of it, okay?

CONSTANCE: I gave him some coffee.

PAUL: Thanks.

CONSTANCE: He looked terrible.

PAUL: I know how he looked.

CONSTANCE: What do you do, give him money?

PAUL: Sometimes.

CONSTANCE: Does he have somewhere to stay? I mean it's snowing out.

PAUL: *I* don't know.

CONSTANCE: Where does he go when it gets really cold?

PAUL: Acapulco.

They work in silence.

I'm done here.

CONSTANCE (*finding a small packet at the bottom of a drawer*): You won't believe this.

PAUL: What is it?

She hold up the packet for him to see.

I don't believe it. *Rubbers*? Let me see.

CONSTANCE (*giving him the packet*): Can you believe it?

PAUL: I mean this guy couldn't cut his own food.

CONSTANCE: Hope springs eternal. You want 'em?

PAUL: You're a riot. Hey, I gotta go.

CONSTANCE: Where? North wing?

PAUL: South. Mrs. Swenson's in the mood for a bath.

CONSTANCE: Mmmm. Go get her, Bearclaw.

PAUL *stops in his tracks, glares at* CONSTANCE.

Okay, okay. Paul.

PAUL: See you at lunch.

CONSTANCE: Thanksgiving lunch.

PAUL: Yeah. Turkey loaf.

PAUL *exits.* CONSTANCE *finds one sock and a pair of suspenders in the last drawer. She puts them into the bag. She makes a final survey of the room, clipboard in hand. When she is finished, she tears off the top sheet on the clipboard, crumples it into a wad and tosses it into the wastebasket. The lights drop to the level of a winter afternoon.*

A voice on the public address system: 'Sheryl, call for you on line 13. You got a call, Sheryl, please pick up 13.'

Scene Two

PETER *dressed in an overcoat, opens the door.* CONSTANCE *reads from the next sheet on her clipboard.*

CONSTANCE: Asgard, Peter T.

PETER: Ahs-gard.

CONSTANCE: Ahs-gard. Well, It really is one of the nicest. Of course, it's small . . .

PETER: Oh, no, this is going to be all right.

CONSTANCE: Those glass doors go out to your own little terrace.

PETER (*starting down toward the doors*): Terrific.

CONSTANCE: They're locked. Regulations.

PETER (*stopping*): Of course.

CONSTANCE: In the summertime we unlock them. It's really pretty out there. Trees . . .

PETER: I can imagine.

CONSTANCE (*indicating*): Lots of closet space.

PETER: Great.

CONSTANCE: Bath, easy chair, writing desk, straight-backed chair, motorized bed . . .

PETER: My Lord, I wouldn't ever have to leave this room. (*She looks at him.*) Ah-hah. I guess that's the point.

CONSTANCE: You look too young to be here.

PETER: I suppose I am, relatively.

CONSTANCE: Well, there's all kinds of activities . . . (*Beat.*) I have this feeling you're not really big on bingo.

PETER: No, no, no . . . it's all fine. I chose this place myself.

CONSTANCE: Oh.

PETER: I chose the room for the light.

CONSTANCE: Well, there certainly is a lot of it, during the day.

PETER: I'm a Sunday painter.

CONSTANCE: Really?

PETER: Drawings, mainly. Charcoal sketches, pastels. I just started last year.

CONSTANCE: Take off your coat, why don't you.

PETER: I'm working my way up to primitive.

CONSTANCE (*helping him off with his coat*): Well, you'll have to draw me some day. (*She puts his coat on a hanger and hangs it in the closet. While she's in the closet,* PAUL *enters carrying a poinsettia.*)

PAUL (*to* PETER): Hi.

PETER: Hello.

PAUL: Mr. Asgard?

PETER: Ahs-gard.

PAUL: For you.

PETER: You shouldn't have.

CONSTANCE *emerges from the closet.*

CONSTANCE: This is Paul, one of our orderlies.

PETER: How do you do.

PAUL: Where do you want it?

PETER: I'd rather you kept it.

PAUL: Reception says it's from your son.

PETER: I know, I know. It's the sort of thing that would make this place look like a hospital room. You keep it, Paul. Really.

CONSTANCE: Don't be silly. It's for you.

PETER: I don't care for poinsettias. They've never had an appeal for me. Bah, humbug, I say to this poinsettia.

PAUL: I think it's nice.

PETER (*a flash of anger*): Then keep it! (*Beat.*) Ah, just put it anywhere.

PAUL *puts the plant on the writing desk and starts to leave.*

PETER: Thank you.

PAUL (*turning back*): Sure. (PAUL *exits.*)

CONSTANCE: Well, unless there's anything I can do for you . . .

PETER: No, not a thing.

CONSTANCE: I want to welcome you, Mr. Asgard. You're going to like it here, I know.

PETER: I've ordered newspaper delivery, several of them. When will that start?

CONSTANCE (*consulting her clipboard*): Let me see. Well, well. Quite a list of them. You speak all those languages?

PETER: Temporarily.

CONSTANCE: No kidding. Well, I suppose you could have the local papers beginning tomorrow, but some of these others may take a few weeks to get going.

PETER: Fine.

CONSTANCE: All set, now?

PETER: All set.

CONSTANCE: Okay, then. Five-thirty in the cafeteria for supper.

PETER (*dismayed*): Five-thirty!

CONSTANCE: I'll check in on you later.

She exits. PETER *looks about him for*

a moment. *He picks up the poinsettia, looks for another place to put it, and then wearily puts it down on the writing desk again. He picks up the card from the plant, puts on reading glasses, and sits at the desk. He reads the card. He puts it back in the plant and takes off the glasses. He sits in the twilight that comes in through the glass doors.*

A voice on the public address system: 'Hello, hello! It's Monday night, and that means bingo. Seven-thirty in the north-wing lounge – bingo lovers, unite!'

Scene Three

The light fades rapidly. The door opens and PAUL, *carrying a dinner tray in one hand, switches on the overhead light with the other.*

PETER (*with a start*): What? Who's there? What is it? Turn off that light!

PAUL *sets the tray down on the bed, switches off the overhead light, and goes to* PETER. *He puts his hands on* PETER's *shoulders.*

PAUL: Hey. It's okay.

PETER: Don't touch me!

PAUL: It's okay. You're gonna be okay.

PETER: Don't touch!

PAUL *takes his hands off* PETER's *shoulders.*

PAUL: All right.

PETER: Who are you?

PAUL: I'm Paul. Remember? (PAUL *switches on the desk lamp, and* PETER *looks up into his face.*)

PETER: No. No, I don't. Where am I?

PAUL: You're in the home, Mr. Asgard. (*Beat.*)

PETER: Oh. (*Pause.*) Oh, yes. The Home.

PAUL: You missed supper. I brought a tray for you.

PETER: And you're an orderly here.

PAUL: More or less. Do you want something to eat?

PETER: I remember now. I remember you.

PAUL: Shoot. I'm unforgettable. How about something to eat?

PETER: No. No, thank you.

PAUL: You gotta eat.

PETER: How's the food?

PAUL: Tonight? Awful.

PETER: In that case, no thanks.

PAUL: I'm afraid I can't take no for an answer. (PAUL *goes and brings the tray from the bed to the desk.*)

PETER: I see, I see. You're a fascist.

PAUL: Sure. But I'm a cute fascist. (PAUL *sets the tray down and uncovers it.*) God, are you in luck. Fish-patties.

PETER: I didn't remember you at all. For a moment there, I had no memory of this place, or coming here, or any of it.

PAUL: Creamed corn, french fries, prune juice, you'll love it.

PETER: And now I remember it all.

PAUL (*picking up a fork and offering it*): Come on, Mr. Asgard. Eat up.

PETER: Look! I do not yet need to be fed!

PAUL: Okay. Feed yourself. (*Pause.*)

PETER: I just don't want everybody being suddenly solicitous all over me.

PAUL: Don't worry. I won't be. What is that? Solicitous?

PETER: Ah . . . concerned. Overly concerned.

PAUL: No problem.

PETER: The doctors say I have to expect these lapses of memory. Get used to them, they say. Get used to them!

PAUL: What's wrong with you?

PETER: Nothing's wrong with me! (*Beat.*) I had an accident.

PAUL: Yeah?

PETER: That's actually what they call it. Cerebral vascular *accident.* Like I stepped on a banana peel.

PAUL: You had a stroke.

PETER: Not bad, moderate. Year and a half ago. The only lingering effect was a little trouble with the right side of my body. (*Talking out of the side of his mouth:*) Talked like this for awhile, you know? Like Jimmy Cagney. (*Normal voice:*) So, I got into physical therapy, started drawing, worked my way back to near-normal. *But.* The medications the doctors pump into me are scrambling my brains.

PAUL: What are they giving you?

PETER: Coumadin and Centrax.

PAUL: Oh, God. What's the Centrax for?

PETER: To 'reduce behavioural problems.'

PAUL: Behavioural problems?

PETER: Ten milligrams, two to three times daily.

PAUL: Oh, boy. A regular trouble-maker.

PETER: I can't live without the junk, and I can't live decently with it. At home, I'd find myself in the kitchen without a clue where the bathroom was. The connections in my brain simply disconnect.

PAUL: What a total fuck.

PETER (*with a laugh*): Yeah. Well put. You don't notice it at first. At first you just say to yourself, Now where did I put those damn keys, or . . . or you're talking to someone and the right word is there on the tip of your tongue and that's exactly where it stays.

PAUL (*genuine*): Oh, my God. That sounds just like me. (PETER *laughs.*)

PETER: I hope you'll call me Peter.

PAUL: I mean it, that sort of stuff happens to me all the time.

PETER: Listen: I don't think you've got anything to worry about.

PAUL: Easy for you to say. (*Indicating the tray.*) You're not going to eat any of that crap, are you?

PETER: Nope.

PAUL: It's not always this bad.

PETER: I hope not.

PAUL: If I cover for you tonight, you gotta promise to eat every damn thing they give you tomorrow. Promise?

PETER: Fascist! From the Latin word,

fasces. A symbol of power in ancient Rome. A symbol of authority. It was a bundle of sticks with a single axe projecting out of them. You see? Fascism: A lot of little sticks supporting one big stick.

PAUL: Oh, that helps a lot. You talk like a teacher.

PETER: History.

PAUL: College?

PETER: High school.

PAUL: I knew there was something about you I didn't like. Which high school?

PETER: Southwest.

PAUL: Rich kids' school.

PETER: You?

PAUL: South.

PETER: Poor kids' school.

PAUL: That's me. Do you mind if I smoke? I'm not allowed to smoke on the floor, but . . .

PETER: It's a destructive habit. And expensive. And pointless. Go ahead. (PAUL *produces his ashtray, fits it on his finger, pops it open and lights a cigarette.*) Remarkable.

PAUL: Nice, huh?

PETER: Mankind has come a long way. High school. Did you graduate?

PAUL (*bristling just a little*): Yes, I graduated.

PETER: What have you been doing since then?

PAUL: What does it look like? Clawing my way to the top.

PETER: Do you plan on going to college?

PAUL: No.

PETER: Why not?

PAUL: I just don't.

PETER: You're not planning to spend your life doing this?

PAUL: I don't know. After a while you get sort of attached to bedpans.

PETER: That's no attitude.

PAUL: It's one attitude. Come on, what is this?

PETER: You came here straight from high school?

PAUL: No. Look, they'll be paging me in a minute.

PETER: What else did you do?

PAUL: Worked.

PETER: Doing what?

PAUL: God, get you going, you don't stop!

PETER: What did you do?

PAUL: Sold men's clothes.

PETER: Where?

PAUL: Fitzroy's.

PETER: Exclusive store.

PAUL: I suppose.

PETER: So? You had a job selling men's wear in a fashionable shop. What happened?

PAUL: What do you mean, what happened? Nothing happened.

PETER: You quit.

PAUL: Sure.

PETER: They fired you?

PAUL: Jesus!

PETER: What happened?

PAUL: I fell in love with the merchandise, okay?

PETER: I see. You stole.

PAUL: God, I'm loving this. It's like high school all over again.

PETER: You didn't like high school?

PAUL: Stop! Enough! No more questions!

PETER: Just trying to get to know you.

PAUL (*rising to leave*): Yeah, right. I'll see you around.

PETER: Look, I'm curious, that's all.

PAUL: Curious! You're like a dentist with a drill!

PETER: So were you arrested, or what?

PAUL: Oh, your students must have loved you, man.

PETER (*defensive*): My students did love me.

PAUL: Yeah? So where are they? Where's

the wife, the kids, the students who loved you so much? People don't usually check into this place alone, you know.

PETER (*angry*): I wanted to do this on my own! It was my idea, wise-guy.

PAUL (*after a beat*): Sorry.

PETER: I insisted!

PAUL: I'm sorry.

PETER (*after a pause*): My wife passed away. I have a son. (*Pause.* PETER *beginning to drift.*) My students ... Students are transient.

PAUL: What's that? Transient? (*Beat.*) Peter? What's your son's name? (*Beat.*)

PETER: What?

PAUL: Are you feeling okay?

PETER: There's a boy ... Very small. He has my name ...

PAUL: Who's this, your grandson?

PETER: A sailor-suit. Blue. And a white cap and he's standing in a boat ...

PAUL: This is your grandson, right? (*Beat.*) Peter?

PETER: *Never* stand up in a boat, dammit!

PAUL: I'll go get the nurse, Mr. Asgard.

PETER: Never!

PAUL (*shaking* PETER): Peter?

PETER (*looking up at* PAUL): Do I know you?

PAUL: Sure you do.

PETER: You're sure?

PAUL: You know me. I'm Paul, your orderly.

PETER: Orderly?

PAUL: Your friend. South High School.

PETER: Oh. Oh, yes.

PAUL: Paul, remember?

PETER: Poor kids' school.

PAUL: Now you got me. (*Pause.*) You gonna be all right?

PETER: When I forget, it's like a window opens at night, a round window, the porthole of a ship, maybe, and outside there's just a circle of deep dark blue.

PAUL (*after a pause*): No stars?

PETER: It's very quiet out there.

PAUL: You feeling better now?

PETER: Oh, sure. It just opens and closes.

PAUL: Well, I gotta go.

PETER: It's blurry out there. Murky. Like some painting by Turner. Do you know Turner?

PAUL: I know Tina Turner.

PETER: Jospeh Mallord William Turner was a great English painter. Most of his works hang in a London gallery called the Tate. Seascapes. Interiors. Murky.

PAUL: Right. Sure. Well. Do you want the nurse?

PETER: Whatever for?

PAUL: Good question. Okay, then.

PETER: You'll come back?

PAUL: Don't worry.

PETER: I'll tell you all about fascism.

PAUL: Oh, Great. History lessons. (PAUL *picks up the tray.*)

PETER: Goodnight.

PAUL *exits, carrying the tray.* PETER *stands, takes off his jacket and tie, and drapes them over the back of his chair. He sits again. After a moment he switches off the desk lamp.*
A voice on the public address system: 'Paging Dr. Lindholm, please. Dr. Lindholm, please pick up a house phone.'

Scene Four

Three weeks later, the room is filled with mid-morning light. PETER *stares at his watch, bewildered and frightened.* CONSTANCE *knocks at the doors and enters, followed by* PETER Jr.

CONSTANCE: *Here* we are.

PETER Jr.: That's him, all right.

PETER: Peter. Good morning.

CONSTANCE: Another Peter!

PETER Jr.: Junior.

CONSTANCE: Right, right. You haven't been here before.

PETER Jr.: He didn't permit me.

CONSTANCE (*picking up* PETER*'s jacket and tie*): No kidding.

PETER Jr.: I guess he was a little touchy at first. About being here.

CONSTANCE: But he's adjusting so *well*.

PETER: And he's here, present in the room, and can be addressed directly. (*Pause.*)

CONSTANCE: Right. (*Beat.*) Well. I'll see you Peters later.

PETER Jr.: Goodbye.

She goes.

Have you been waiting long?

PETER: Waiting? Oh, yes, you've thrown off my schedule for the entire day.

PETER Jr.: Sorry.

PETER: I may have even missed the bingo. (*Beat.*) What time *is* it?

PETER Jr.: A little after eleven. (PETER *looks at his own watch.*) Your watch stop?

PETER (*listening to his watch*): No, no, it's not that.

PETER Jr.: How are you doing?

PETER: Pretty well. No complaints.

PETER Jr.: That would be a first. You like it here?

PETER: It takes some getting used to.

PETER Jr.: They treating you all right?

PETER: Oh, yes. Nice people.

PETER Jr.: And the other residents?

PETER: Old. Very old.

PETER Jr.: What did you expect?

PETER: I don't know that I expected anything. (*He looks at his watch again.*) A little after eleven you say?

PETER Jr.: Why the mystery, Dad?

PETER: Mystery?

PETER Jr.: All of this – on your own. You didn't have to give up the house, you know. You just . . . didn't have to do it.

PETER: How else could I pay for this place?

PETER Jr.: I would have helped you, you know that. Anyway, you don't belong here.

PETER: I do now.

PETER Jr.: You're too young to be here.

PETER: For how long am I too young? A matter of months? A year?

PETER Jr.: Well, then, come and live with us. Fran would welcome it, I would welcome it, we'd both feel so much better about it all.

PETER: A man has to face the realities of his situation, and adjust to them, that's something I always tried to teach you.

PETER Jr.: And I'm telling you we're ready to make the necessary adjustments, we would do any amount of adjusting.

PETER: And I would have twenty-four-hour-a-day witnesses to my decline.

PETER Jr.: Witnesses? I'm your son, for God's sake!

PETER: It's easier this way, easier all around.

PETER Jr.: Never give an inch.

PETER: I'm doing it this way for your sake as well as mine.

PETER Jr.: Never let anyone else give an inch.

PAUL *appears at the door, carrying a tray of medications.*

PETER (*noticing* PAUL): Here they're neutral. I'm just part of the job.

PETER Jr. (*not wanting to go on with this in front of anyone*): Dad . . .

PETER: Ah, Paul? This is Peter, my son, the lawyer. Peter, meet Paul, my friend, who is at present working as an orderly. Until he discovers what it is he's *supposed* to be doing.

PAUL: Hi.

PETER Jr.: How are you.

PAUL (*to* PETER): Your medications.

PETER: Oh, good. For the falling-apart.

PETER Jr.: What are they giving you these days?

PETER: Glue. (PAUL *laughs alone, then falls silent.*)

PETER Jr.: You know it's going to be no problem to and from this place to ours, getting here and back, I checked it out on the map and you just take Highway 12 right on into the city, through the loop till you link up with 194 and then it's straight shot across the river all the way to the Summit Avenue exit.

PETER (*swallowing a pill with water from a white paper cup*): You took Summit?

PETER Jr.: Wait a minute. Was it Summit? No.

PETER: Como.

PETER Jr.: Como, of course! Right.

PETER: What about Lake Street?

PETER Jr.: Lake Street?

PETER: You avoid the freeways with Lake Street.

PETER Jr.: Well yes, sure.

PETER: Get on Excelsior Boulevard right there in St. Louis Park, it turns into Lake Street ...

PETER Jr.: Straight shot down Lake into the city ...

PETER: Across the Lake Street bridge and keep on going when Lake turns into Marshall all the way to Summit.

PETER Jr.: To Summit, sure.

PETER: Of course, if you were in a hurry, you wouldn't *want* to avoid the freeways.

PETER Jr.: No, no, right.

PETER: But you could still take Lake to 31st and pick up 135, take 135 to 194, across the river to St. Paul and all the way to Como. (PETER *takes another pill.*)

PETER Jr.: I'll try that. I'll definitely give that a try.

PETER: You wouldn't have to mess with Highway 12 at all.

PETER Jr.: I hadn't thought of that.

PETER: But if *I* were doing it, I'd take Excelsior to Lake to Marshall to Summit to Como.

PAUL: Where would you park?

PETER: In the lot. (*Realizes* PAUL *is having him on.*) Wise guy.

PETER Jr.: You will spend Christmas with us, won't you?

PETER: Oh, yes. Of course. Yes. Thank you. And thanks for the plant.

PETER Jr.: You liked it?

PETER: I liked it.

PETER Jr.: Great, I'll just keep them coming then. So. Pick you up Thursday afternoon?

PETER: Why?

PETER Jr.: Christmas Eve.

PETER: Oh. Oh, yes. We're not exchanging gifts, are we?

PETER Jr. (*after a pause, controlled*): It had entered my mind.

PETER: You mean you've already gone and got something for me? Dammit, you know how I feel about that!

PETER Jr.: It's something people do for each other, this time of year. The holly and the ivy. You've heard of it?

PETER: It seems so pointless among adults ...

PETER Jr.: Dad, do not get started on that.

PETER: What the hell am I supposed to give you? Or your wife, for that matter?

PETER Jr.: From you she doesn't expect a thing!

PAUL: I'll come back later ...

PETER (*to* PAUL): You stay put!

PETER Jr. (*to* PAUL): Don't worry, I'm on my way out.

PETER (*to* PETER Jr.): You want me to make something for you in occupational therapy? A napkin holder, maybe?

PETER Jr.: We are not talking about Christmas presents here, is that obvious to everyone?

PAUL: I'll see you all later ...

PETER (*to* PAUL): You're not going anywhere!

PETER Jr.: Dad. This is ridiculous. A

drawing. One of your sketches.

PETER: They're not good enough.

PETER Jr.: Geez! A gesture. That's all it's about. Gestures.

PETER: Christmas gifts in a home without children make no sense.

PETER Jr.: At last! *This* is what we're talking about!

PAUL (*to* PETER): I thought you had a grandson.

PETER: I should be so lucky.

PETER Jr.: Dad . . .

PETER: They *choose* not to have children, that's the point.

PETER Jr.: Dad, we do not have to go into this in front of . . . in front of . . .

PAUL: Paul.

PETER Jr.: Paul.

PETER: Children *redeem* a household.

PETER Jr.: Private! This is private! (*Silence.*) I'm sorry. (*To* PAUL:) Really. This is nothing. Just a well-rehearsed two-step. (*Beat.*) Forgive us. (*Beat.*) We're sorry, right Dad? (*Beat.*) Right. (*To* PETER:) No gifts this year, okay?

PETER: Well, if you've already gone to the trouble . . .

PETER Jr.: No gifts! Just us. And a wonderful meal.

PETER: I suppose I could pick up something or other here in the gift shop . . .

PETER Jr.: No gifts! (*Beat.*) Please. You'll come?

PETER: Sure. Of course.

PETER Jr.: Spend the night with us. Spend as long as you want. All right?

PETER: Thursday, then.

PETER Jr.: Right. (*To* PAUL:) Take good care of him, okay?

PAUL: I'll try.

PETER Jr.: And don't let him give you any of his crap.

PAUL: Now that's asking a lot.

PETER Jr.: Bye, Dad.

PETER: Thursday.

PETER Jr. *goes.*

PAUL: You guys should be on T.V. (*Offering a paper cup of pills and a paper cup of water.*) Come on, Mr. A. Bottoms up. I've got other pills to push.

PETER: Don't go. Please. I'm . . . a little anxious.

PAUL: What's up?

PETER: Look at this. (*He extends his arm and shows his wristwatch.*) My watch. Look. (PAUL *looks at* PETER's *watch.*)

PAUL: Yeah?

PETER: It doesn't mean a thing to me. I look at it and I see it and I see the face and I remember *watches* and *clocks* but it doesn't mean a damned thing to me, big hand, little hand, Paul, I can't tell time anymore, I can't tell what time it is.

PAUL (*after a pause, putting his hands on* PETER's *shoulders*): What a total fuck.

Blackout.

Scene Five

From down the hall, the sound of an elderly senile resident calling out, 'Mavis?' again and again. The lights rise on PETER *in bed,* CONSTANCE *standing above him, taking his blood pressure. Evening. The poinsettia is gone: A crocus stands in its place.*

PETER: That old man is going to drive me out of my mind.

CONSTANCE: He can't help it.

PETER: 'Mavis, Mavis.'

CONSTANCE: He's calling his wife.

PETER: Well, why the hell doesn't she answer!

CONSTANCE: She's dead.

PETER: Great. That's just great. I end up in a loony bin.

CONSTANCE: After this last stunt of yours, you are in no position to talk.

PETER: Stunt?

CONSTANCE: Those people wanted to play bingo, they did not want to hear a lecture on the Industrial Revolution.

PETER: I thought they were a very appreciative audience.

CONSTANCE: Anyway, your doctor has increased your Centrax as a result. Is that what you wanted?

PETER: My doctor is nearly senile himself.

CONSTANCE: He knows what's best for you.

PETER: How long is this going to take?

CONSTANCE: As long as I say.

PETER: Viva il Duce.

CONSTANCE: Do I smell smoke?

PETER: My blood pressure is nowhere near that high. Are you about finished with me?

CONSTANCE: Yes, thank God. (*She unwraps the band from his arm.*)

PETER: What's the verdict?

CONSTANCE: You'll live.

PETER: You sound disappointed.

CONSTANCE: You *don't* have cigarettes in here, do you?

PETER: An expensive habit, and filthy, and pointless.

CONSTANCE (*hanging the clipboard on the end of the bed*): All right. Just holler if you need anything.

PETER: *I* do not holler. Mavis's *husband* hollers. Can't you shut the door to his room?

CONSTANCE: If I do I won't be able to hear him.

PETER: If you don't, I *will* be able to hear him!

CONSTANCE: Goodnight, Mr. Asgard. (*She exits.*)

PETER (*after a pause*): The coast is clear! (*The bathroom door opens, and PAUL sticks his head out.*)

PAUL: God. She nearly caught me. (PAUL *enters the room.*)

PETER: What do you expect? The air in here is blue.

PAUL: Blue? I had one cigarette.

PETER: And that's one too many.

PAUL: Didn't you ever smoke?

PETER: Certainly I did. Corn silk behind the corn crib.

PAUL: Too much, man.

PETER: Yes, it was, as a matter of fact. Got sick as a dog and never tried it again.

PAUL: Kind of a dare-devil, weren't you?

PETER: Lippy. A lippy boy. Anyway, there's no need for you to smoke in class.

PAUL: In *class*!

PETER: I mean . . . You know what I mean.

PAUL: Look, Peter, I'm off duty, I'm hungry, I've got a friend waiting for me at home.

PETER: Now, where was I before we were interrupted?

PAUL: God. World War I.

PETER: World War I. So. Strictly speaking, fascism was born out of the social and economic chaos which followed the first world war. Believe me, the time was ripe.

PAUL (*lighting a cigarette*): You were there, right?

PETER: I'll ignore that. The various growing fascistic movements found recruits easily enough from the ranks of three main classes.

PAUL: What was your wife's name?

PETER: What? Hannah. Three main classes, each of which was nurturing its own particular grievance: One, the defeated military. Two, a generation of frustrated youth.

PAUL: How did you first meet?

PETER: Who? Hannah? Church social. These were kids who had been too young to fight in the war, and who were attracted by fascism's two-pronged thrust: Violent action, and the all-embracing leadership of a single charismatic figure.

PAUL: When did she die?

PETER: A long time ago. Someone to tell

them what to do, and when and where and how. Someone who knew *what was best for them*.

PAUL: How long ago?

PETER: Pay attention, will you? Before you were born. Am I wasting my breath here?

PAUL: No.

PETER: All right. Finally, number three, the single most dangerous group of them all: The vast disenfranchised middle class. Why dangerous, you ask?

PAUL: I didn't, but . . .

PETER: Simple. Inflation. When there's a universal pinch in the pocket, nothing's uglier than the mood of the shopkeeper, the bureaucrat, the lawyer, the truck driver . . .

PAUL: The schoolteacher.

PETER: The schoolteacher. Most of them have worked for what they have with a single-mindedness which has closed them off to any of the other compensations that make living on this planet worthwhile: an appreciation of beauty, nature, travel, the arts, you name it. Inflation robs them of the only thing they possess in their stunted value systems.

PAUL: Not pretty.

PETER: They feel cheated, but they don't know who it was who cheated them, they don't know whom to blame. What does it lead to?

PAUL: I give up.

PETER: Anger. Racism. Bigotry. Persecution. When people feel the presence of an enemy, but don't know who or what it is, what do they do?

PAUL: They get scared.

PETER: Go to the head of the class. Exactly! They get scared. (*Pause.*)

PAUL: I gotta go, Peter, I'm late already.

PETER: Fine, fine. So who's this friend waiting for you?

PAUL: A friend, all right? My roommate.

PETER: What's his name?

PAUL: Joe. Joe.

PETER: Joe the fellow who picks you up after work?

PAUL: You don't miss a thing, do you.

PETER: He drops you off in the mornings, too.

PAUL: He's an early riser.

PETER: What's that little car he drives?

PAUL: An Audi, and yes, he should have bought American.

PETER: Do you have relations with this fellow?

PAUL: What?

PETER: You know what I'm talking about. I was a schoolteacher for thirty years, I've seen it all, believe me.

PAUL: I'll bet you have.

PETER: So you are queer then.

PAUL: Jesus! (*Beat.*) You don't approve?

PETER: Oh, it's none of *my* business.

PAUL: Hah!

PETER: How did you meet?

PAUL (*sullen*): Church social.

PETER: Wise guy. What does this Joe fellow do for a living?

PAUL: He writes for the paper.

PETER: Which one?

PAUL: *The Dispatch*.

PETER: Well, that's something, anyway. (PAUL *lights another cigarette.*) Didn't you ever try it with girls?

PAUL: God. Yes. Sure.

PETER: So what went wrong?

PAUL: Nothing went wrong!

PETER: It didn't work? You didn't like it?

PAUL: It worked! I liked it!

PETER: I guess I don't understand.

PAUL: No, I guess you don't. (*A knock at the door.*) God. (PAUL *quickly stubs out his cigarette and disappears into the bathroom.*)

PETER: Who is it?

CONSTANCE *opens the door.* PETER Jr. *stands behind her, a cookie tin in his hands.*

CONSTANCE (*musical*): Surprise, surprise.

PETER Jr. (*entering*): Hi, Dad.

PETER: Peter.

PETER Jr.: So. How about some cookies?

PETER: Cookies?

PETER Jr.: Sure. I made this huge batch after dinner. Fran was at the health club for the evening and I was all alone and feeling kind of hungry and so I said to myself, Why not? And I just sort of got going and kept on going and I ended up with a few dozen more than I ever intended, so I thought why not just hop in the car and bring you a crateful. (*Beat.*) Peanut butter.

PETER: None for me, thanks.

CONSTANCE: Not right now, thanks.

PETER Jr.: Right. So how are things?

PETER: Couldn't be better. They're turning me into a junkie.

PETER Jr.: More Centrax?

CONSTANCE: He gives us no choice.

PETER (*with some pride*): You heard about my *cause célèbre*?

PETER Jr.: Ah, the lecture? I did hear something . . .

PETER: The word spread like wildfire. The walkers were clattering up and down the halls, dentures were cracking . . .

CONSTANCE: You really got a kick out of it, didn't you?

PETER: It beats bingo.

CONSTANCE: Did you ever think how *they* felt? Carl Lundquist's card was nearly full when you took over the microphone, he was in tears.

PETER: Look: When Paul finally hauled me out of there I got a round of applause!

CONSTANCE: The applause was for Paul! (*She is at the bathroom door.*) Okay, Smokey the Bear, you can come out now. (*After a pause,* PAUL *emerges, sullen and embarrassed.*)

PETER Jr.: My God. What the hell is going on here?

PETER: We were going over a few of the elements of fascism.

CONSTANCE: Smoking again, right? Am I going to have to report you to the supervisor, Paul?

PAUL: I gotta go.

PETER: He's got a date.

PAUL (*to* PETER): You shut up about that!

PETER Jr.: Now look here, Buster . . .

PAUL: Get out of my way.

PETER: Don't keep your date waiting. (PAUL *exits, slamming the door behind him.*)

CONSTANCE: Paul! (*On her way out, to* PETER:) You! Are more trouble than you're worth! (*She exits.*)

Long pause.

PETER Jr.: Your blood pressure still up?

PETER: They don't tell me a thing.

PETER Jr.: I know the feeling. (*Gesturing toward the bathroom door.*) You got any more in there? Like clowns out of a Volkswagen, one hundred and forty-six orderlies come tumbling . . . He's getting to be a regular, isn't he?

PETER: He's getting to be a regular pain in the neck.

PETER Jr.: Remember when you found out I smoked? You told me to stop so I did but the only way I could was to chew a lot of gum, and then you told me what sugar would do to my teeth. I switched to sugarless. He talks to you?

PETER: What? Paul? Ach. Kids. Thinks he's in love. *You* know.

PETER Jr.: He comes in, talks, smokes, you counsel him, sort of?

PETER: It's difficult to break the habits of a lifetime.

PETER Jr.: God, don't I know it. (*Beat.*) I see you got the crocus.

PETER: Yes. Thanks. It's lovely.

PETER Jr.: Like this one habit of mine. Trying too hard. You know? After Mom died. I tried too hard, didn't I?. *You* know. With you. Worked at it too much.

PETER: What are you talking about?

PETER Jr.: The habits of a lifetime. Like. When I was in school, second year, I fell in love with this British girl, law student, black hair and white skin. Deirdre, can you believe it? And it was a total mistake from the word go. You mind if I talk here, for a minute?

PETER: Go right ahead.

PETER Jr.: I start taking her out. Dinner, walks along the Esplanade, in the Public Gardens. And it's all fine. She likes me well enough. She talks, she listens. A little pre-occupied, maybe, but she listens. The same in bed.

PETER: Peter . . .

PETER Jr.: A little pre-occupied, but she's there, anyway. Sort of. What isn't fine about it all is that her . . . reserve . . . is driving me totally out of my head. The cooler she gets the hotter I get. Crazy. Completely. I'm beginning to make a fool of myself, trying too hard, calling her, seeing her, giving her things, I can't keep my hands off her . . .

PETER (*overlapping*): Peter, please . . .

PETER Jr. (*overlapping*): . . . which is a mistake, of course, I know that, everybody knows that, but I can't help myself. Every time I make a vow to let her alone, I break it. And by now she's avoiding me for all she's worth, making up excuses, *hiding* from me, and I just keep bashing my head against the wall, and I wonder, what's wrong with me? (*Beat.*) You won't believe what I did.

PETER: What did you do?

PETER Jr.: I got a can of bright green spray paint one night, and on the sidewalk right outside her dorm I wrote in huge letters, 'I AM A PIG FOR YOU, DEIRDRE.' (*Beat.*) She never spoke to me again. (*Beat.*) So what was wrong with me? That I kept on trying when I knew it was no use?

PETER: I don't know.

PETER Jr.: Neither do I. (*Beat.*) I'll leave the cookies here. (*He sets the box on the writing desk and exits. Slow fade to black.*)

After a moment, in the darkness, a voice on the public address system: 'Hello, hello! The semi-finals of the Scrabble tournament will begin promptly at six-thirty in the north wing lounge. Coffee and cake are being served by the ladies of the Naomi Circle, and all pocket dictionaries will be checked at the door. This means you, Mr. Lundquist. Now, go get 'em, all you semi-finalists!'

Scene Six

In the darkness, 'Goodnight, Irene' on the harmonica. The lights rise on PETER and PAUL. PETER is doing a charcoal sketch of PAUL, who poses with a harmonica to his lips, occasionally playing it. The crocus has been replaced by a large Easter lily.

PETER: The trouble with van Gogh was, van Gogh didn't believe in himself. (*Pause. PETER sketching.*) He didn't. No matter how brilliant you and I may know he was, he wasn't buying it. That was his tragedy. Every man has his own tragedy, and that was his.

PAUL: So he took a pair of scissors and cut his ear off.

PETER: Part of it.

PAUL: I wonder: why the ear?

PETER: Don't move around like that.

PAUL: Why not the hand he painted with, or a finger, at least, if he thought he was so bad?

PETER: Come on, Poetry-in-Motion, hold still.

PAUL: Maybe he figured he'd heard enough.

PETER: All that talent, that vision, but when he looked at himself, he just couldn't see it.

PAUL: When *I* look at myself, I don't even *think* about amputation.

PETER: Well, Paul, that's why I like you. (*Long pause: PETER sketching, PAUL playing 'Goodnight, Irene' on his harmonica.*) Paul. What's your last name, anyway? (*Pause. PAUL continuing to play the harmonica.*) What's your last name? (*Beat.*) Paul?

PAUL: That's it. Just Paul.

PETER: Don't give me that. What's your last name?

PAUL: What's up? You want to call me on the telephone?

PETER: Oh, come on. What is it?

PAUL: Paul. Just Paul, okay?

PETER: Okay, okay. (*Pause.*) Know why I have you posed like that? With your harmonica?

PAUL: I give up.

PETER: I'm afraid of your lips. Your mouth. Eyes, ears, nose and throat I can do, no problem, but a mouth – that's another doctor.

PAUL: Coward.

PETER: I suppose so. Tell you another secret.

PAUL: Yeah?

PETER: Hands are a total bitch. But the way you cup them around that harmonica, like they're one solid ball, it's a breeze.

PAUL: Are you telling me you don't believe in yourself?

PETER: What a little wise-guy you turned out to be.

PAUL: He doesn't believe in himself. Hide the scissors.

PETER: When I first met you, little did I know. (*Pause,* PETER *sketching.*)

PAUL: Peter?

PETER: Yes?

PAUL: I've decided to take your advice.

PETER: How so?

PAUL: I'm gonna take some classes.

PETER (*putting down his sketch pad*): Well. That is simply the best news I've had in a long, long time. Good *going,* Paul.

PAUL: Thanks.

PETER: Thank *you.* What are you going to study?

PAUL (*genuinely proud*): Water-colour painting and karate.

PETER (*after a beat*): What did you say?

PAUL: In Hawaii.

PETER: Hawaii.

PAUL: I'm sick of these winters, man. And I met this guy who's a travel agent and he says there are some great charters going to Hawaii and he's gonna get me some brochures.

PETER (*anger rising*): Water-colour painting and *karate*?

PAUL (*a little defensive*): You said water-colour had to be one of the biggest challenges you could face.

PETER: And *karate*?

PAUL: I'm sick of being defenseless, man.

PETER: Of all the utterly *stupid* . . . I urge you to get a grip on your life, and you decide to . . . I don't believe it. This is not my advice you are taking. This is some drugs you are taking, it has to be!

PAUL (*hurt*): I thought you'd be proud.

PETER: Proud? Proud? You are a hair-brain! A fluff-head!

PAUL: Cut it, okay?

PETER: Dizzy!

PAUL: Just cut it! It was only an idea, anyways . . .

CONSTANCE *enters, carrying a newspaper.*

CONSTANCE (*musical*): Hello, hello!

PETER (*grim*): Hello, Sunshine.

PAUL (*to* PETER, *sullen*): It was just a thought, for God's sake.

PETER (*to* PAUL): Take my advice: Don't think.

CONSTANCE: Sounds like we're having a *swell* time. That German newspaper you ordered?

PETER (*taking it*): *Die Zeit*? I don't believe it.

CONSTANCE (*looking over* PETER's *shoulder*): Say – that is really pretty good.

PETER: Thank you.

CONSTANCE: No – I mean it.

PETER: It never occurred to me you didn't mean it.

CONSTANCE: A little condescending this morning, aren't we. Paul, you had a visitor.

PAUL: Oh, God.

CONSTANCE: It's okay. I gave him some coffee.

PAUL: He's gone?

CONSTANCE: Yup. Oh, and Joe's been on the phone for you, and the beds in the south wing haven't been made up yet.

PAUL: Right. Thank you.

PETER: And thanks for the paper. It's only three months old, you know.

CONSTANCE: You can always look at the pictures, Asgard. (*She exits.*)

PETER: Whoops.

PAUL: You treat her like she's stupid or something. She's not.

PETER: I know that. She's a mental giant. So who's this visitor of yours? (*He tosses the newspaper aside.*)

PAUL: My accountant. How long is this gonna take?

PETER: The trouble with you is, you're not willing to put a little effort into the things you do.

PAUL: Yeah, that's my tragedy. (*Pause. PETER sketching.*)

PETER: Roger Hecht. Class of '68. When I first got hold of that boy he was completely nowhere. A total disaster. Didn't know who he was and didn't care.

PAUL: I got this feeling you set old Roger straight.

PETER: Damn right I set him straight! I opened his eyes to himself. Showed him that the road he was on was nothing but an absolute dead end, no question. I let him know that there were worlds out there he never dreamt of: Art, history, philosophy, music, uplifting books . . .

PAUL: How did old Rog feel about all this?

PETER: I'll tell you exactly how he felt. He felt grateful. To me. For the two years that I had him, I didn't let up on that boy for one minute.

PAUL: Dear God.

PETER: Hey, sit still.

PAUL: What's this guy up to now? Wait. Don't tell me. He's an astronaut.

PETER: Roger Hecht is now a very well-respected member of his community. Hold your pose, for God's sake.

PAUL: What does he do?

PETER: I got a Christmas card from him. Four, maybe five years ago. Photo of the family. Nice looking wife, three beautiful little girls. Maybe it was six years ago . . .

PAUL: For a living, what does the guy do? To support all those women?

PETER (*sketching, after a pause*): He sells lawn furniture.

PAUL: Oh, that's great!

PETER: Will you put that harmonica back in your big mouth!

PAUL: You give old Rog the world on a platter, and he ends up peddling lawn furniture. And all he's good for is one lousy card in all these years? That's really good.

PETER (*after a pause*): And the son of a bitch was only trying to sell me a patio suite. (*After a beat, the two of them laugh together.*) Terrible skin! In thirty years of teaching history to acne victims, old Rog was the worst! (*They laugh again, fall silent, and PETER continues to sketch while PAUL plays the harmonica.*) But that doesn't alter the point I've been trying to hammer home with you. Not by a jot.

PAUL: Paul, you gotta go to college. Paul, you gotta take life seriously. Paul, you gotta make something of yourself.

PETER: Yes, yes, and yes.

PAUL: Paul, trust me: I know what's best for you.

PETER: Well, maybe, just maybe, I do.

PAUL: Trust me, Paul: I know what's best for everybody.

PETER: You *want* to be stuck in this place for the rest of your life?

PAUL: Well, *you* are, goddammit! Maybe I don't have any more choice than you! (*Beat.*)

PETER: You can't hurt me that easily, if that's what you're after.

PAUL: Shit. I'm sorry.

PETER: It'll take a lot more than a little lip from you to get me going.

PAUL: Jesus, though, you're always riding me, you never let up.

PETER: It's for your own good.

PAUL: Exactly! You know everything! You have an education, you've travelled overseas, you speak all those languages, so of course, you know all about me!

PETER: What I know about is the infinite potential of every single one of God's creatures.

PAUL: Oh, great. Now he's a missionary.

PETER: 'Little lamb, who made thee? Dost thou know who made thee?'

PAUL: Dear God.

PETER: The man who wrote those words was an artist, and you can see his drawings hanging in one wing of . . .

PAUL (*overlapping*): Of the Tate Gallery in London, England.

PETER (*overlapping*): . . . the Tate Gallery in London, England. William Blake. He had a vision, and he followed it. That's all I'm trying to say to you. Find your vision. Follow it.

PAUL: Yeah. Right. Session's over.

PETER: Paul?

PAUL: God, I'm stiff.

PETER: Please.

PAUL: This little lamb is a little short on cash. Makes it hard to move, much less follow a vision.

PETER: That's bullshit.

PAUL: Bullshit? I don't have the money to go to college! I don't have the brains! And besides, I don't fucking want to!

PETER: Pure bullshit. Brains, you don't have to worry about, you've got more than enough. And you don't want to only because you're afraid to. As for money, that's just a question of discipline. How do you spend the money you make here?

PAUL: Jewellery, mostly. Now and then a fur coat.

PETER: Sure, be a wise-guy.

PAUL: What do you think I make for hauling old folks' shit all day? For lifting Mrs. Swenson and carrying her to the toilet? For coming home at night with piss all over my whites? I should be making a fortune. Guess what: I don't.

PETER: What about this Joe fellow? Would he help you?

PAUL: He owns too much of me already. Besides he's barely getting by as it is.

PETER: Are your parents in a position to help at all?

PAUL: My father is in the position of being dead. My mother's got three little kids to take care of, okay?

PETER: I'm sorry.

PAUL (*still angry*): Don't be.

PETER: Your father must have been very young. When did he pass away?

PAUL: Many moons ago.

PETER: Come on, Paul. How did he die?

PAUL: Forget it.

PETER: How?

PAUL: Forget it, I said.

PETER: I want to know!

PAUL: God. (*Beat.*) He was a fireman. There was a fire.

PETER: I'm very sorry.

PAUL: Yeah.

PETER: Wait a minute. Wouldn't your mother be receiving benefits? Pension? Insurance?

PAUL: It's not enough.

PETER: How old were you when it happened?

PAUL: I don't know. Twelve.

PETER: Twelve. (*Beat.*) Well. There you have it. Something to strive for. Something to live up to. The memory of your father.

PAUL (*very angry*): Dear God, will you give me a break! Just shut up, will you!

PETER: Don't talk to me like that.

PAUL: You? You can't even talk to your own son without getting constipated!

PETER (*also very angry*): Now you hold it right there!

PAUL: You can't talk to him, he can't talk to you, put the two of you in a room together, you get instant constipation, both of you!

PETER: How dare you!

PAUL: Mister Fucking Know-it-All!

PETER: You're shackled, you're in chains!

PAUL: To me, you're just part of the job!

PETER: I'm telling you, you're too scared to live!

PAUL: And I'm telling you, you are a total fuck!

PETER: Get out!

PAUL: I'm going!

PETER: Don't come back!

PAUL: Don't worry! (PAUL *goes out, slamming the door.* PETER *picks up the Easter lily, opens the door, and flings it out into the hall. He slams the door and goes to the bed. He droops, sits slowly on the bed, and puts his head into his hands.*)

Scene Seven

The lights shift to a night-time blue, coming in through the glass doors. PETER JUNIOR *enters, followed by* CONSTANCE, *who carries a vase of bleeding-hearts.*

PETER: Hannah? Hannah, is that you? Hannah?

PETER Jr.: How long has he been like this?

CONSTANCE: Off and on for about a week.

PETER: Where is he, Hannah?

PETER Jr.: He's talking to Mom.

PETER: Hannah?

CONSTANCE: It's me, Mr. Asgard. Connie. Constance. You know that.

PETER: Hannah, where's that boy who used to visit?

CONSTANCE: Who?

PETER: What's become of him?

CONSTANCE: You mean Paul? He's still around. He's got the night shift now. You're probably asleep when he's on duty.

Beat.

PETER: Let's go camping this summer, like we used to.

CONSTANCE: Oh, God.

PETER: Bay Lake, Pelican, Whitefish, Trout Lake. We wouldn't have to go tenting, I know that was a burden for you, we could rent a cabin.

CONSTANCE: Peter.

PETER: We could be tourists for a change, instead of trail-blazers, what do you say?

CONSTANCE (*after a beat*): I think that sounds just fine, Peter.

PETER: Was I hard on you, Hannah? A little overbearing, maybe?

PETER Jr. (*grasping* PETER's *shoulders*): Dad.

PETER: A little bossy?

PETER Jr.: Dad?

PETER: What. Peter? What.

PETER Jr.: How are you doing?

PETER: When did you get here?

PETER Jr.: Just now. How are you feeling?

PETER: Ach. Little woozy. Stuff they give me before bed. Packs a punch.

PETER Jr. (*to* CONSTANCE): Can't they ease up on those damned pills a little?

CONSTANCE: When we do he starts wandering off, all over the building.

PETER: 'Wandering off.' Used to be when I went somewhere I was 'going places.' It's late, isn't it?

CONSTANCE: A little after eleven.

PETER Jr.: I stayed late at the office getting that stuff about Paul you asked for.

PETER: What? Oh. Oh, yes. Thank you.

CONSTANCE: What stuff about Paul?

PETER Jr.: Oh, you know, his background, family records, that sort of thing.

PETER: Look, she does not have to hear about . . .

PETER Jr.: My office has a department that investigates insurance claimants, so Dad asked me to check out this Paul.

CONSTANCE: If you wanted to know about him, why didn't you just ask him?

PETER Jr.: Ask *him*.

PETER (*taking the portfolio from PETER Jr.*): If you will excuse me, I would like to retire now.

CONSTANCE: Be my guest, I got off at eleven anyway.

PETER: In that case, goodbye.

CONSTANCE: Oh, come on, Asgard. I'll help you. (*She begins to unbutton his shirt.*)

PETER: Please. Let me. (PETER *begins unbuttoning his shirt, slowly and with difficulty.*)

CONSTANCE: I'll get the cuffs, they're always a problem.

PETER (*flailing at her*): Will you please just . . .!

CONSTANCE: Okay, okay. (*Long pause. At first* PETER Jr. *and* CONSTANCE *watch as* PETER *struggles laboriously and unsuccessfully with his buttons. When it becomes embarrassing, they both turn and look out the glass doors.*)

PETER Jr.: Won't be long now, you can get out onto the terrace.

CONSTANCE: Oh, it's wild, everything just blooming away.

PETER Jr.: You know I actually had to mow the lawn this week?

CONSTANCE: No kidding. Already?

PETER Jr.: It was that long.

CONSTANCE: Wow. Already.

PETER Jr.: Take your sketch pad out there, your charcoals. Did you know he's half Indian?

CONSTANCE: Paul?

PETER: Indian?

CONSTANCE: Well, sure. His name is Bearclaw, for God's sake, did you think he was French?

PETER: Bearclaw.

CONSTANCE: On the floor we call him The Gay Brave. (*Beat.*)

PETER Jr.: *Also* he is *gay*?

CONSTANCE: All orderlies are gay.

PETER Jr.: God.

CONSTANCE: You wouldn't be prejudiced, would you?

PETER Jr.: What, me? Oh no, oh no.

CONSTANCE: Most of them are very gentle with the residents, and they spend so much time working out, they're certainly strong enough to do the job. (*Beat.*)

PETER Jr.: You should have an easel for out there on the terrace. How about I pick you up an easel? Have your coffee out there, your morning papers, the crosswords, and then get down to work. What a set-up. About three years ago he was arrested, shoplifting from the store he worked for. Shoes, mainly. A few silk ties, some shirts, mainly shoes.

CONSTANCE: Hey, that's all in the past.

PETER Jr.: What isn't? His father's been in and out of jails for years.

PETER: His father.

PETER Jr.: Drunk and disorderly, for the most part. Some petty theft. He doesn't look it, particularly. Paul. Indian.

CONSTANCE: So have you investigated me, too?

PETER Jr. (*with a smile*): Not yet.

CONSTANCE: That's a relief.

PETER Jr.: You taking all this in, Dad? Or is this nothing new. Dad? (*Long pause.*)

PETER (*finally, still fumbling with his buttons*): My fingers . . . get confused.

CONSTANCE: Well if you'd just let me help you . . .

PETER Jr.: I'll take care of it.

CONSTANCE: You'll get him to bed?

PETER Jr.: Sure.

CONSTANCE: That all right with you, Peter?

PETER: Goodnight.

CONSTANCE: I'll check in on you later. (*She exits.*)

PETER Jr. *begins to unbutton his father's shirt.*

PETER Jr.: Losers. Creeps. All of them. Oh, I'm sure he's a perfectly nice kid. A nice kid, perfectly. So it's not him, is it, Dad. It's why do I spend my life crazy jealous of this long line of losers you pick up? Huh? In your classes, on the street, God knows, the supermarket.

PETER: I stood by you, didn't I? When it looked like you were the loser?

PETER Jr.: Let's get that belt buckle.

PETER: I didn't turn my back on you, not for a minute.

PETER Jr.: Nope.

PETER: Through all the drugs and the crazy screwed-up philosophies, the hair and the clothes and the anger . . . your terrible anger towards me . . . I always let you know that you could come back. Just that. Come back.

PETER Jr.: No questions asked.

PETER: No questions asked.

PETER Jr.: And I came back.

PETER: And you came back.

PETER Jr.: And no questions were asked.

PETER: Nope.

PETER Jr.: Not one. (PETER Jr. *eases* PETER's *shirt off his shoulders.*)

PETER: Peter?

PETER Jr.: Oh, yeah, I was some kind of hippie, wasn't I, Dad. For twelve months, exactly. I did the whole thing by the book, went to San Francisco . . . put some flowers in my hair . . . It was like a junior-year-abroad. (*He drapes the robe over* PETER's *shoulders.*) Okay, off with the pants. (PETER Jr. *slides* PETER's *trousers off.*) I did hold your interest for a while though, didn't I.

PETER: I was never uninterested in you.

PETER Jr.: You cared for the creeps, so I had a fling at being one. Didn't work. Doesn't matter.

PETER: I cared for you always. I still do. It's just that . . . I'm a teacher. It's my calling. And some of those kids were in such need.

PETER Jr.: Where's your pyjamas?

PETER: Look! The physician doesn't tend the healthy.

PETER Jr. (*erupting*): It wasn't my fault! It wasn't my fault I was healthy!

PETER: Peter . . . I never said . . .

PETER Jr.: You said! You said! You didn't say a goddam thing! The two of us locked in that big house together, without her, just two men *looking* at each other all those years. But you never stopped talking to her. I was there, and she wasn't, but she was the one you talked to, God, I tried, I tried, but all I ever heard from you was nothing! (*Beat.*) I was a pig for you, Dad. (*Long pause.*)

PETER: Is it because of me? You don't want children because of me?

PETER Jr. (*weary*): Oh, fuck.

PETER: I screwed up with you, so you don't want to screw up with yours. (*Beat.*) It's because of me.

PETER Jr.: Look. It's still an open question. (*Pause.*)

PETER: I took you away, remember? After? We went away together, Bay Lake, Pelican Lake, Trout, Whitefish, all the old places. From one lake to another, all that summer after she died, don't you remember? The two of us.

PETER Jr.: I remember.

PETER: All that summer. (*Pause.*)

PETER Jr.: She just shouldn't have left us, should she?

PETER: No.

PETER Jr.: We needed her.

PETER: Yes. (*Pause.*)

PETER Jr.: How many languages do you suppose we have, Dad? Between the two of us. Six? Seven? Seven with my Latin.

PETER: I have Latin too, you know.

PETER Jr.: Of course. (*Beat.*) We just never spoke the same one at the same time. (*Long pause. Then* CONSTANCE *knocks at the door, and enters.*)

CONSTANCE: Everything all right in here? (*Pause.*) Let's get you into bed.

PETER Jr.: Yes. You should be going to bed.

PETER: Yes. I need to sleep.

CONSTANCE: I'll take over from here.

PETER Jr.: Okay.

PETER: Peter?

PETER Jr.: Dad?

PETER: Goodnight.

PETER Jr.: Goodnight.

CONSTANCE: I'm going to pull the curtains now.

PETER Jr.: Sure.

She draws the curtains around the bed, and disappears with PETER *behind them.* PETER Jr. *goes to the glass doors and looks out into the night, standing in the same place that* PAUL *has occupied earlier while he smoked.* PETER Jr. *takes a stick of sugarless gum from his pocket, unwraps it, and chews. Finally,* CONSTANCE *tip-toes out from behind the curtains.*

CONSTANCE: Out like a light. In the morning, he'll be clear as a bell.

PETER Jr. (*as they leave the room*): Thanks for all your help. I know you're off duty . . .

CONSTANCE: Thank *you* for all the flowers. You know, bleeding-hearts were my favourites when I was growing up?

PETER Jr.: Yes?

CONSTANCE: Bleeding-hearts and baby's breath. (*They exit the room,* CONSTANCE *turning off the light.*)

A very long pause. Then PAUL *enters the room quietly. He looks at the curtained bed. He walks down to the glass doors and lights a cigarette. He looks out into the night, smoking. The dim light fades to black.*

Scene Eight

In the darkness, a voice on the public address system: 'May I have your attention, please. The representative from H & R Block will be available for tax consultations on Tuesday and Thursday of next week, because it's that time of year again, folks. All those residents who would like a little tax-talk should make an appointment with Sheryl at the nursing station. Thank you.'

Bright early morning light streams in through the glass doors. PETER, *dressed in pyjamas and dressing gown, is poised to sketch* CONSTANCE.

CONSTANCE: So. Do you want me sitting or standing or what?

PETER: Suit yourself.

CONSTANCE: I think I'll sit.

PETER: Why don't you stand?

CONSTANCE: I'd rather sit.

PETER: If you insist. (*She sits.*) All it took was a little research and a couple of phone calls.

CONSTANCE: Don't you think you should let Paul in on this?

PETER: If the Bureau of Indian Affairs is passing out scholarships, why shouldn't Paul get one? He certainly qualifies. But don't you breathe a word about this to Paul. I want to surprise him.

CONSTANCE: My lips are sealed.

PETER: He comes in here when he thinks I'm asleep. I can smell the smoke.

CONSTANCE: And you don't say anything?

PETER: We're not speaking.

CONSTANCE: Well, if you're not speaking, how are you going to surprise him? (*Beat.*)

PETER: This is going to be very difficult.

CONSTANCE: What is?

PETER: Can't you put something in front of your mouth?

CONSTANCE: *What?*

PETER: You could wear one of those surgical masks.

CONSTANCE: What on earth are you talking about?

PETER: I have a little trouble drawing the human mouth, d'you mind?

CONSTANCE (*rising*): Well if you think I'm gonna sit here wearing a *mask* for God's sake . . .

PETER: It doesn't have to be a mask necessarily . . .

CONSTANCE: This is my *portrait* you're doing!

PETER: Sit down!

CONSTANCE: Why? I thought you

wanted me standing!

PETER: I don't particularly want you at all, if it comes to that! (CONSTANCE *starts to leave.*)

CONSTANCE: It's no wonder Paul asked for the night shift.

PETER: You! Stop! Right there, young lady! (CONSTANCE *stops. Beat. She turns back to face* PETER, *smiling in spite of herself.*)

CONSTANCE: Young lady? One minute I could choke you, the next ... *Young lady*? Asgard, I'm yours.

PETER: If at first you don't succeed, quit, this is your motto, all of you.

CONSTANCE *sits.* PETER *regards her. He gets the vase of bleeding-hearts and puts it in her hands.*

CONSTANCE: Now we're getting somewhere. When I was a teenager, bleeding-hearts were very big with me. I don't think you ever fall in love again quite so hard. Or so hopelessly. (PETER *is in position with his sketch pad, scrutinizing her.*) And at that age, heartbreak is part of it all, somehow. Heartbreak. Love wouldn't be the same without it.

PETER: Hmmmmm.

CONSTANCE: My father grew a row of these in the back garden, along the driveway. Bleeding-hearts and baby's breath. Eventually you trade one for the other.

PETER: A little less talk?

CONSTANCE: Yeah. Right. (*Beat.*)

PETER: Mm-mm. No. (*He goes to her.*) You're breathing them, get the picture? Their aroma.

CONSTANCE: But bleeding-hearts don't have an ...

PETER: Just ... do it.

CONSTANCE: Yes, sir. (*She smells the bleeding-hearts.*)

PETER: More like this. (*He positions the vase of flowers so that it obscures her face, and then goes back to his sketch pad.*)

CONSTANCE (*after a pause, deliberately*): You have completely covered up my face, have you not.

PETER: Oh, I wouldn't say completely ...

CONSTANCE (*rising*): Well, anyway, we tried.

PETER: Wait a minute! I'm not giving up that easily. If at first you don't succeed, quit. Take you, for instance. All this medical training in your background. Did you ever consider taking it a step further? Did you ever once consider becoming a doctor?

CONSTANCE: No.

PETER: There, you see? So easily contented. So easily defeated.

CONSTANCE: *Defeated*?

PETER: Pamela Braunschweiger, class of '72. Classic non-achiever. Small dreams. I'm telling you, this girl's dreams were minute! *And.* She was a gum-snapper. What do you want out of life, Pamela? Snap. What do you hope for? Snap. What do want to make of yourself? Bubble, scratch, check the fingernails, snap! I mean this girl enacted the entire story of her life within her own oral cavity! (*Beat.*) Stop laughing, it's no joke.

CONSTANCE: Yes, sir.

PETER: Okay. Sure. So she was overweight. (*Beat.*) You're laughing again.

CONSTANCE: I can't help it.

PETER: That's what Pamela said. I can't help it. I'm fat now, I always have been fat, and I always will be fat. Snap.

CONSTANCE: And?

PETER: *And*, I got that girl on the most austere diet in the history of diets. I got the gum out of her mouth, and some decent food into it, and not too much of it. Okay. It was a start. I spent every lunch-hour for six months in the student cafeteria. I practically had to sit on her, but I did it.

CONSTANCE: Congratulations.

PETER: Thank you.

CONSTANCE: But I never wanted to be a doctor. I always wanted to be a nurse. It's that simple. I'm doing exactly what I always wanted to do. And I'm loving it. I wouldn't call that a defeat.

PETER: You're married?

CONSTANCE: Was.

PETER: Divorced?

CONSTANCE: Yup.

PETER: If at first you don't succeed . . .

CONSTANCE: We're talking about things that are none of our business now, aren't we?

PETER: Any kids?

CONSTANCE: A girl.

PETER: Fatherless.

CONSTANCE: Okay, Jack, let's put the lid on it, shall we? I don't know what planet you come from, but here on mine some things work out and some don't, and nobody really has a lot of control over either. And if you haven't learned that by now, when will you? (*Beat.*) I was married before I graduated from high school, for God's sake. I was a child. (*Beat.*) You're in such a hurry to give people The Word. Like. You're in such a hurry to get Paul out of here. Okay. He's an orderly. Not glamorous, not lucrative. But he works hard. He's good with the people. He's good *for* the people. So where do you get off making him feel miserable for *that*? Huh? (PETER *is silent.*) You know, in this place, I shouldn't say it, but it's true, people come and people go, and some you notice and some you don't, and that's just the way it is. You – you, you notice. You're the resident sore thumb, as a matter of fact, and with that poor kid of yours limping around here all the time with his flowers and his cookies and his *face*, Jesus! Scrubbed and shining and giving you chances right and left and you miss the boat every damned chance you get!

PETER (*pained*): I am not unaware . . .

CONSTANCE: Well, Jack, when you're a *nurse*, you have many duties, and one of the things you get to do as a *nurse* is, you get to count the comings and the goings and you get to count the chances that people get and I'm telling you *already* you've had more than your share. What does a *nurse* do? She tells you time's up. (*Beat.*) I've got to go now. (*She goes to look at the blank page of the sketch pad.*) Well, there's one thing anyway. At this point you could go almost anywhere with it. (*She exits.* PETER *does not move.*)

A voice on the public address system: 'Sheryl, we need you in 203 immediately. Sheryl, please report to the south wing immediately.'

Scene Nine

The lights fade to night-time levels, and then rise slightly with the first glimmer of dawn. After a pause PAUL enters quietly. He does not notice PETER sitting in the bed, partly obscured by the bedside curtain. PAUL stands looking out the glass doors. He produces his ashtray and lights a cigarette. Long pause.

PETER: You really shouldn't smoke.

PAUL: God. (*Beat.*) I didn't mean to wake you.

PETER: You didn't wake me.

PAUL: Oh. Good.

PETER: What time is it, anyway?

PAUL: I don't know. Dawn.

PETER: No, you didn't wake me.

PAUL: Well. I guess I'll shove off.

PETER: Well. If you have to.

PAUL: I just came in to check on things.

PETER: You come in here to smoke, night after night. (*Beat.*)

PAUL: That's not why I come in here.

PETER: No?

PAUL: Tell the truth, I missed talking to you.

PETER: You should take those cigarettes and throw them out the window.

PAUL: That's what I missed. Advice.

PETER: Oh, God, just can't stop, can I? Well, I'm swearing off it. No more advice. For anyone, ever.

PAUL: That's a long time, Peter. (*Beat.*)

PETER: It's been a while.

PAUL: Over a month.

PETER: So how have you been?

PAUL: Oh, you know.

PETER: No, I don't know, that's why I asked – oh, God, there I go again.

PAUL: Hey, it's okay.

PETER: Grilling you. I know what's going to happen. I'll die. That's a given. And with any luck I'll make my way up to St. Peter and he'll say, 'How you doin', old fella?' And I'll say to him, 'Look at yourself. Wasted potential. One of the most famous saints in history, and you end up a doorman.'

PAUL: Talk about wasted potential. You should have been on T.V. (*Beat.*) So how *are* you doing?

PETER: Pretty well. Given there's a little time-bomb somewhere in my brain, ticking away, I'm doing pretty well. How was your night?

PAUL: Mrs. Swenson died.

PETER: Oh.

PAUL: I was with her.

PETER: Oh.

PAUL: Yeah. Old Tons of Fun. I'm gonna miss her.

PETER: You know what time is, Paul? You want me to tell you? Time is a total fuck. (*Beat.*) Now you listen to this because it's the very last piece of advice I'm ever going to give anybody.

PAUL: I knew you wouldn't last.

PETER: I'm serious. You've got to stop denying your name, you've got to stop denying your father, you've got to find him, the two of you have to find each other, and you've got to do it while there's still time. (*Pause.* PAUL *is stunned.*) You have a beautiful last name. (*Beat.*) Bearclaw. Beautiful. (*Beat.*) It's a little unusual, isn't it, a white woman marrying an Indian?

PAUL: Chippewa. Mom has a mind of her own. Did he show up here?

PETER: No.

PAUL: Then how did you . . .? I won't ask. Anyway you probably figured by now he wasn't a fireman, he didn't die, he's out there somewhere, drunk as an Indian.

PETER: He's your father.

PAUL: Tell me about it.

PETER: You've got to talk to each other.

PAUL: You try talking to him.

PETER: Before it's too late.

PAUL: It was always too late.

PETER: Maybe . . . maybe you're just not talking the same language.

PAUL: Yeah? Well I don't know where you go to school to learn that one. (*Beat.*) Beautiful? You think my name is *beautiful*?

PETER: Yes. Yes, it is. And it's yours.

PAUL (*bitter*): Well, it was pretty popular back on the reservation.

PETER: The reservation?

PAUL: You know, the bearclaw is a very big thing with us. Because the bear is a very big thing with us. So it stands for all kinds of stuff. But my father told me once, we were sitting in front of the T.V., I forget what we were watching, and he was still sober enought to talk, I don't know, I think I was 12 or something and already he had a pretty good idea I was queer, Indians got a real nose for that kind of thing. Anyway, he said the father bear looks at his cubs and if they're okay he pulls in his claws and gives them a pat and if they're not he puts his claws out and rips them open. (*Beat.*) I think it was 'Bowling for Dollars.' (*Pause.*)

PETER: Oh, dear God. (*Beat.*) There are scholarships available to Indians, Paul. You could get one, you're eligible.

PAUL: Forget it, Peter.

PETER: College scholarships.

PAUL: Look. I already tried it. The Bureau of Indian Affairs, they're a bunch of total fucks. You know why they won't give me a scholarship? Because my father never had a birth certificate, can you believe it? They weren't so good at making certificates back on the reservation. And so, Mr. Bearclaw isn't an Indian. He's not Chippewa because according to the BIA he ain't even been born. (*Beat.*)

PETER: There must be other avenues.

PAUL: Hey: I don't know what I'm gonna do. I'll figure it out for myself.

PETER: You grew up on a reservation?

PAUL: No, here in town. But my father did, so we'd go back sometimes. Visit the old family plantation.

PETER: Yes?

PAUL: We'd go ricing. In that part of the country, the Indian is allowed one industry, just one. Wild rice. It was hard work, but I loved it. You go along in a canoe, right through the stalks, and you beat them with sticks, and the wild rice falls into the canoe. It's good money, too, man. I remember once, I was about six years old. I bought a pair of brand-new leather shoes with the money I made ricing. It was my birthday, and that was my birthday present to myself. (*Beat.*) I put those shoes right next to my bed. I kissed the soles before I went to sleep. I was only six, right?

PETER: When's your birthday?

PAUL (*evasive*): What?

PETER: Your birthday. When is it?

PAUL: Many moons. When the rice is in the canoe.

PETER: Wise-guy. I'll find out, just watch me.

PAUL: I don't need leather shoes anymore, Mr. A. Nothing but sneakers from here on in.

PETER: Peter Junior's birthday is coming up.

PAUL: Yeah?

PETER: Oh, I've got something planned for him, don't you worry about that.

PAUL: I thought you didn't like giving gifts.

PETER: Some things you just get out of practice.

PAUL: He's a lot like you.

PETER: Peter? You're out of your mind.

PAUL *reaches for a cigarette, and winces painfully with a stitch in his side.*

PAUL: Ooo.

PETER: What's the matter? You hurt yourself?

PAUL: Yeah, I hurt myself.

PETER: How?

PAUL: It's no big deal, Peter, I just got some tape on my ribs that's driving me crazy.

PETER: You've got your ribs taped up and it's no big deal? What happened?

PAUL: I forgot to learn karate.

PETER: Tell me.

PAUL: A couple of cops tried to flirt with me outside a gay bar. They were a little clumsy. Eat that for breakfast, Mr. Onward-and-Upward.

PETER: But that's appalling. They struck you? Well, we've got to do something. Register a complaint . . .

PAUL: Yeah, right. They'd be delighted to hear from us.

PETER: What were you doing outside a gay bar?

PAUL: I was coming out of it.

PETER: What were you doing *in* the bar?

PAUL: Research.

PETER: Sure, be a wise-guy. How does that Joe guy feel about you going to places like that?

PAUL: I wouldn't know. I don't live with him anymore.

PETER: What?

PAUL: I split.

PETER: You left him? Oh, that's great, just great.

PAUL (*dangerous*): I don't want to talk about this, Peter.

PETER: The one stable thing in your life and you throw it away.

PAUL: I mean it.

PETER: Sure it was weird, but at least it was stable.

PAUL: I thought you weren't going to grill me anymore!

PETER: Why did you do it? So you could go running around to bars?

PAUL: No! No! I don't know why! Because he always had to be on top, how's that? (*Beat.*) He tried to help me. And help me, and help me, and help me. Somebody trying to help you all the time, it gets so you think you need help. (*Beat.*) Like you. This condition you've got? The stroke, the medication, all of it? That's not your tragedy. Your tragedy is you've always gotta be on top! (*Beat.*)

PETER: I hurt everyone I touch.

PAUL: Goddam right you do!

PETER: My students. My wife. You. I've got a son who's afraid to conceive a child because of what I did to him. (*Beat.*)

PAUL: Peter? Now, don't. Just don't, please. What are you crying for?

PETER: I'm not.

PAUL: Come on. Don't. You did help me, you know.

PETER: Bullshit.

PAUL: You did. You just sometimes forget to pull in those claws, that's all.

PETER: I don't know a goddamned thing about helping anybody. I can't even help myself, for God's sake.

PAUL: Now that's bullshit.

PETER: You don't know what happened tonight.

PAUL: So what happened?

PETER: I don't want to talk about it.

PAUL: So don't.

PETER: I wet my bed, that's what!

PAUL: Too much.

PETER: How dare you laugh!

PAUL: Look at it one way, it's kind of funny.

PETER: I wet the bed, goddamnit!

PAUL: You mean you've been sitting here all this time . . . Why didn't you tell me, for God's sake? Peter. What's a little pee among friends?

PETER: Go away.

PAUL: I can't do that.

PETER: If it comes down to this, what's the point of starting? Of doing any of it?

PAUL: Is this advice? Is this my career counsellor talking? (*Beat.*) We'll take care of it, it's no big deal. (*Beat.*) Okay. Today, I'm not peeing my pants. But someday I'm gonna. Are you

telling me I just shouldn't bother with any of it? Because of *that*? (*Long pause.*)

PETER: Don't leave me again, will you? I know I'm impossible . . .

PAUL: Don't worry. I'm sick of the night-shift anyway.

PETER: You'll switch back?

PAUL: Sure. Come on.

PETER: I don't think I can move. My legs feel funny.

PAUL: No problem. We'll just give you a lift into the john, that's simple.

PETER: I don't want anyone else to see me like this.

PAUL: Who's gonna see you?

PETER: Don't let anyone else in the room.

PAUL: Over my dead body anybody gets in here. (PAUL *lifts* PETER *out of the bed.*) Ahh! Goddam tape!

PETER: How are *you* going to keep anyone out, sissy?

PAUL (*carrying* PETER *into the bathroom*): I'll hit 'em with my purse, Peter. I'll hit 'em with my purse.

The dim lights fade to black. In the darkness, a harmonica playing 'Goodnight, Irene.'

Scene Ten

PETER's *bed has been stripped bare. The bleeding-hearts have been replaced by lilacs.* CONSTANCE *and* PAUL *are making the bed from scratch: Mattress pad, sheets, covers, pillowcases. They work in silence. Eventually* PETER Jr. *enters, dressed in a dark suit and carrying a large coffee-table book.*

CONSTANCE: How did it go?

PETER Jr.: Just fine. It was hot out there.

CONSTANCE: I'll bet.

PETER Jr.: A few of his old students showed up.

CONSTANCE: Great.

PETER Jr.: At least, I assume that's who

they were.

CONSTANCE: Pamela Braunschweiger? (PETER Jr. *regards her blankly.*) Never mind.

PETER Jr.: I'm sorry you weren't able to join us.

CONSTANCE: So am I.

PETER Jr.: You said there was a package for me?

CONSTANCE: It was stuck in the back of the closet. (*She goes to get it.*)

PETER Jr.: Ah, Paul? (*He offers the book.*) This was Dad's. (PAUL *stares at him.*) He left a note, you should have it. Turner.

CONSTANCE: Can I see? (*She takes the book, leafs through it.*)

PETER Jr.: He talked like some big-time traveller but he never was. Couldn't afford it. But about ten years ago he went on a little package trip for high-school teachers, toured all over England and Wales. That's when he got this book on Turner, in the gift shop of the Tate.

CONSTANCE: That's this guy? Turner? It's beautiful. (*She gives it to* PAUL, *who takes it and turns to look out the glass doors.*)

PETER Jr.: Well. The relatives are waiting back at the house. Paul? Fran and I would like you to come. (*Beat.*) I would like you to come.

PAUL: I'm on duty.

CONSTANCE: It's nearly three, you can take off early.

PAUL: I can't make it.

CONSTANCE: I'll cover for you.

PAUL: I can't.

PETER Jr.: I know how you feel, Paul, but I hope you'll come.

PAUL: Please don't tell me you know how I feel. You don't, okay?

PETER Jr.: I can try, can't I?

PAUL: He was about the best thing ever happened to me. (*Beat.*)

PETER Jr.: Yeah. I guess you're right. I don't know how you feel. (*Beat.*)

CONSTANCE (*offering the envelope to* PETER Jr.): Open it.

PETER Jr.: What?

CONSTANCE: It says on the envelope: 'Birthday; Peter Junior.'

PETER Jr.: Ah, my birthday isn't for a week.

CONSTANCE: I think it'll be okay. (PETER Jr. *opens the envelope, pulls out several pastel drawings, and leafs through them.*) Look at that. About two, three weeks before the stroke he started doing pastels. Really pretty good.

PETER Jr.: I remember that suit. That's me.

CONSTANCE: That little boy standing in the boat?

PETER Jr.: I remember that day. I wasn't far out from shore, but I started goofing off and ended up in the water. Dad jumped in and swam out to me, grabbed on and towed me back to the beach. It was a hot day, Pelican Lake. We sat on the sand, drying off in the sun.

PAUL: He drew your mouth.

PETER Jr.: He had a little trouble with it, didn't he. (PETER Jr. *contorts his lips into a comical grimace for a moment.*)

PAUL: He never drew anyone's mouth.

PETER Jr. (*looking at the drawing*): I wasn't goofing off. I just stepped off that boat to see what he would do. He was always best if he thought you were sinking. (*Immediately, to* PAUL:) You coming?

PAUL: Look how I'm dressed.

PETER Jr.: You're very good at what you do. I think you're dressed just right.

PAUL: I won't fit in.

PETER Jr.: Oh, for God's sake, who does?

CONSTANCE (*to* PETER Jr., *picking up the vase of lilacs*): You want these?

PETER Jr.: You keep them.

CONSTANCE: Well. Peter.

PETER Jr.: Thanks for everything, Connie.

CONSTANCE (*on her way out*): I'll see

you tomorrow, Paul. (*She exits.*)

PETER Jr.: You want to ride with me?

PAUL: I've got a car here.

PETER Jr. (*giving* PAUL *a calling card*): Okay, here's the address. Now you get on 135 at the Como entrance, take it to 194, take 194 to . . .

PAUL: Hey. I'll find my way.

> PETER Jr. *looks at* PAUL, *and then exits, carrying the packet of drawings.* PAUL *holds the book tightly to him and looks out the glass doors. After a moment he reads the calling card. The lights fade.*

CRACKS

For Drey Shepperd

MARTIN SHERMAN was born in Philadelphia and educated at Boston University. From 1976-77 he was resident playwright at Playwrights Horizons in New York. He now lives in London. His plays include *Next Year in Jerusalem, Passing By* (Almost Free Theatre, London, 1975 and included in *Gay Plays: Volume One*), *Cracks, Rio Grande, Bent* (Royal Court and Criterion Theatres, London, 1979, plus Broadway and productions in over thirty countries) and *Messiah* (Hampstead and Aldwych Theatres, London, 1983). His latest play is *When She Danced*.

Cracks was first performed at the Eugene O'Neill Theatre Center, Waterford, Connecticut on 31 July 1975, with the following cast:

RICK	Ben Masters
SAMMY	Joe Grifasi
NADINE	Rosemary De Angelis
JADE	Meryl Streep
CLAY	Ed Zang
GIDEON	Christopher Lloyd
MAGGIE	Jill Andre
ROBERTA	Louis Giambalvo
IRENE	Jill Eikenberry

Directed by Tony Giordano
Designed by Peter Larkin

The British premiere was at the Coliseum Theatre, Oldham on 10 October 1981, with the following cast:

RICK	Michael Atkinson
SAMMY	Cliff Howells
NADINE	Susan Brown
JADE	Noreen Leighton
CLAY	Charles Haggith
GIDEON	David Kitchen
MAGGIE	Maggie Ollerenshaw
ROBERTA	Andrew Hay
IRENE	Lesley Nicol

Directed by Dion McHugh
Designed by Robert Jones
Lighting by Bernie Howe

Cracks

In the autumn of 1973 I was in Taos, New Mexico where The Harriet Wurlitzer Foundation, an organization devoted to providing a retreat for young artists, had installed me in a house so I could experience the 'soothing calm' of my surroundings and hopefully write a play. Outside my house lay an astonishing physical and emotional landscape that featured breathtaking canyons and gorges and the Rio Grande – God's country, surely – and ancient Indian pueblos and Indian magic and Indian ceremonies and a sacred mountain forbidden to the white man and a fiercely alcoholic and unhappy Mexican community and an occasional sound of gunfire and wandering tribes of shell-shocked hippies mourning the sixties and a secret Catholic cult named Penitentes who each Easter crucified one of their members. New Mexico, in fact, has a singular law outlawing crucifixion. In this soothing calm, I wrote *Cracks*.

Taos *was* calm compared to The Eugene O'Neill Playwrights Foundation in Waterford, Connecticut where, in the summer of 1975, *Cracks* was first performed. The O'Neill is a unique testing ground for new plays and a rare and positive nurturing experience for young playwrights. For four bizarre weeks the entire American theatre swoops down onto 'Camp Eugene' and creates drama as intricate and heady offstage as on. *Cracks* was performed by a thrilling cast. The audience laughed and laughed. It caused a sensation. Although the O'Neill is supposed to be immune to commercial considerations, people kept dropping out of trees screaming 'smash hit, smash hit' at me. For someone whose work had been totally ignored until then, all this tree dropping seemed a bit surreal. But I did suddenly have many new friends. And dinner invitations. Back in New York strangers smiled at me on the street. Did I really hear them murmuring 'smash hit, smash hit'? I could even get a table at Joe Allens.

Cracks opened off-Broadway at the Theatre DeLys the following winter. The producer was a fiery Spanish beauty with titian hair, fractured English and an impressive bank account that at that stage of her life permitted her to produce plays and at a later stage landed her in prison for fraud. A not unnatural progression.

The first preview went reasonably well. There was work to do, but we had a week. Everyone seemed pleased – except our producer. 'Ze audience, zey laugh, zat is no good', she complained. 'But it's a comedy', the director replied. 'No, no, eet is serious drama. Eet has message', said the producer. 'I have good idea. We hire two actors. Zey dress like newsboys and run down aisles during interval carrying newspapers and shout 'Extra, Extra – read all about eet and zen zey read out ze message of ze play'. She never did reveal what she assumed the message was, but she did solemnly promise us that 'by opening night, zhere will be no laughter'. That was possibly the first promise our producer ever kept.

The week that followed was harrowing. The highpoint occurred when the producer presented a twelve year old student who was 'interested in theatre' and had ideas for rewrites. Neither his ideas nor the newsboys were accepted, but then there was no need – my own rewrites, conceived in confusion and mounting chaos, were horrific enough. The director, loyal and loving to the play, had to spend most of his energy coping with the tantrums of the producer, and the cast, morale diving, became steadily unsteady. At each performance, the audience laughed less.

Opening night. I lay in a back aisle, coiled in a foetal ball, listening to the stunning, spectacular sound of silence. You could hear a pin drop. You shouldn't hear pins drop in comedies. The reviews the next day would have embarrassed Klaus Barbie. Never let a New York critic smell blood. The smash hit was a disaster. My new friends rushed back into the genie's bottle, clutching the dinner invitations. People actually crossed over the road rather than speak to me. I wasn't even allowed into Joe Allen's bar. Such is failure in New York. The experience proved profitable when years later I had a 'success' in the same city. By then I knew that it mattered not if they were throwing confetti or tomatoes

– the best thing to do was to duck and get on with it.

Cracks had a curious survival instinct. One year after the DeLys *débâcle*, Robert Moss, the courageous and idiosyncratic founder of Playwrights Horizons, then a young off-off-Broadway theatre, offered to present the play again. A revival! So *Cracks* opened for a second time in New York to perfectly reasonable reviews from a different set of critics. And in 1980 it had its British premiere at the Coliseum Theatre, Oldham, with a particularly fine company of actors.

Still, scars are scars. I could never forget the silence at the DeLys. I started writing plays where it was proper for an audience to be quiet. I tended not to mention *Cracks* when people asked me about past work. But there have been through the years a handful of people who have remained doggedly partisan to the play through all its rollercoaster history, have stepped on my hand whenever it's been about to burn the manuscript and have outshouted my memories of silence, and none more devoted than Judy Mauer, Geraldine Sherman, James Hammerstein and Gale Garnett (a brilliant Nadine in the first New York production). My knowledge of their delight in finally seeing this play in print only enhances my own.

Finally – my presence in this volume and indeed the very existence of this anthology are due partially to the visionary influence of Drew Griffiths, a gentle man who was ungently removed from our lives one year ago. There is a little bit of Drew here as I write this now and there always shall be.

Martin Sherman

ACT ONE

Scene One

RICK *is alone onstage.*

He is twenty-nine. A wild face, beautiful, a sinewy body.

He is almost naked.

He takes a stick of white make-up and paints the area around his right eye white.

He draws a jagged orange line down his chest.

He colours his loins green.

He wraps a purple sash around his body.

He puts a silver bracelet on one arm, a golden bracelet on another.

He drapes a necklace of turquoise and coral on his chest.

He takes a knife and slits his arm, beneath the golden bracelet, and covers his neck with blood.

He smiles.

He holds his hands out – in supplication – then brings them together and claps twice.

His right leg moves out to one side. His left leg to the other side. A dance has begun.

His face is bathed in ecstasy.

A shot rings out.

RICK *falls to the ground, dead.*

Blackout

Scene Two

The lights rise on RICK's *house. An early summer evening. California, 1973.*

Party sounds are heard coming from the garden, which can be slightly glimpsed, off right. A doorway leads from the garden to the living room, which is stage right. The living-room is well-spaced, comfortable, surprisingly uncluttered. A few rather bizarre paintings hang on the walls. A staircase, upstage centre, leads to the second floor. A window is next to the stairway.

RICK's *study adjoins the living room. A door leads from the living room to the study. Another door, in the study, far left, leads to a bathroom. There are two bay windows in the study, which open to a veranda. All the windows in the house are open.*

The door from the living room to the study is closed. RICK's *body lies on the floor of the study.*

A man and a woman waltz into the living room from the garden. He is thirty-one, long-haired, very Jewish looking. She is twenty-eight, exceedingly vulnerable, with haunted eyes. There is no music. They hum a waltz to themselves in light accompaniment, dance around the room, and off again, into the garden.

JADE *enters. She is seventeen, dressed in feathers and jewellery.*

CLAY *follows her in. He is thirty-eight, distinguished looking.*

JADE: You know what I did the first time I met Rick? It was in my father's house. I was fifteen. My father was producing Rick's television special. I took Rick into my room, and we smoked two joints, and he was just standing there in the doorway, and I did something I'd never done before, I took off all my clothes, and lay on the couch and played with my body, and he said 'I don't believe you're doing this' and I kept rolling over and I got up and went to him and he had a whopping hard-on, so of course we had mad sex, and afterwards, he took me out and bought me a hot-fudge sundae, and then I went home and read some spiritual books for a couple of hours, before I went to sleep. (*Looks around the room.*) Where is he?

CLAY: He's busy. I'd like to get my camera. I'd like to put you on tape. Alright? (*He smiles and takes her hand. They leave.*)

GIDEON *enters. He is thirty, kind of freaky, very stoned. He sits on a sofa and lights a joint.*

The dancers return, waltz around the room again, still humming, and waltz off.

MAGGIE *enters. She is forty-two, garishly dressed, and somewhat dramatic. She carries a glass of egg-nog.*

MAGGIE: Is Rick in his study?

GIDEON: He's working.

MAGGIE: I want to see him.

GIDEON (*takes her hand*): Ahh, let him be.

MAGGIE: You were looking at me.

GIDEON: When?

MAGGIE: Before.

GIDEON: Maybe.

MAGGIE: I know you find me attractive. But just now, Rick's all I can handle. He goes down on me and everything. My last boyfriend didn't go down on me. He wasn't normal. (*She wanders off, into the garden.*)

ROBERTA *enters. ROBERTA is forty-five, and appears to be a man, a rather bulky man, but he is wearing a prim skirt and blouse, and his hair is in a neat little bun. He smokes a cigar.*)

ROBERTA: Rick? Hey, Rick, where the fuck are you? The party is getting rowdy. If you don't come out soon, I'm gonna bust a few heads. (ROBERTA *returns to the garden.*)

IRENE *enters. She is twenty-nine, dressed more sedately than the others.*

IRENE: Where's Rick?

GIDEON: Rehearsing a new number.

IRENE: Gee, in the middle of a party?

GIDEON: That's his way. (*Holds out the joint.*) Want some?

IRENE: No thanks.

GIDEON: You don't like it here?

IRENE (*smiles*): Oh, it's what I expected.

The couple dance in again. Once more around the room, and they stop, laughing. The man – SAMMY – bows to the woman – NADINE.

NADINE: Thank you. I had a wonderful time. (*her voice assumes another tone:*) I was bored. (*her natural tone:*) Oh, shut up. (NADINE, *embarrassed,*

returns to the garden. SAMMY *watches her leave.*)

SAMMY: *Very* weird. (*to* IRENE:) Want to dance?

IRENE: There's no music.

SAMMY (*to* GIDEON): How about you?

GIDEON: Nah.

SAMMY: You've got a pretty ass.

GIDEON (*smiles*): Hey, man . . . thanks.

IRENE (*to* SAMMY): Is it true that . . . (*Stops herself.*)

SAMMY: What?

IRENE: You know.

SAMMY: It's true.

IRENE: It doesn't make sense. I can't picture you entering a monastery.

SAMMY: Because I'm Jewish?

IRENE: Gosh. That's the least of it.

ROBERTA *enters, agitated.*

ROBERTA: Where is the shmuck? People are driving the wrong cars home. I'm gonna lay someone out.

MAGGIE *enters.*

MAGGIE: Cool it, Roberta. Party's almost over. I'll make you a drink.

MAGGIE *goes to the bar.* JADE *and* CLAY *enter.* CLAY *is carrying a video-tape camera and camera-lights with him.* JADE *goes to* IRENE.

JADE: You're Rick's cousin, right?

IRENE: Right.

JADE: Want to come to my room?

IRENE: I don't think so.

JADE: I'm really into families.

NADINE *enters.*

NADINE: Everyone's gone. Where's Rick? (*In her other tone:*) Who cares? (*Her natural tone:*) I care.

Suddenly there is a rumbling sound. The lights flicker, go off, come on again. The entire house seems to be shaking. Then, just as suddenly, it stops.

MAGGIE: Oh my God! What was that?

CLAY: It's alright. Just a slight tremor. No harm.

IRENE: No harm? The whole room shook.

GIDEON (*hands her a joint*): Here.

NADINE: It happens a lot.

IRENE: You people are crazy, living in this place.

JADE (*walks to study*): Rick, did you feel the earthquake? (*Opens door, enters study.*) Rick?

GIDEON: Leave him alone.

JADE (*sees the body*): Rick . . .

IRENE: I mean, aren't you all afraid of dying? I could never live here. It doesn't make sense.

JADE (*kneeling over the body*): Rick . . .

CLAY: You get used to it.

JADE (*returns to living room*): Hey, it's very heavy in there. Rick's dead.

Blackout

Scene Three

A light shines on JADE's face. It is a few minutes later. The light comes from the lights attached to CLAY's camera. CLAY is filming JADE.

CLAY: Jade.

JADE: Once, I wanted to be a dancer. My father sent me to ballet school. I practised every day. But then I had a spiritual revelation, and I stopped dancing, because, you see, it's easier to fuck. Fucking is easier than writing a poem, cooking a meal or weaving a rug, all of which I wanted to do at one time. Fucking is easier than falling in love. It means you're living in the now – no future, no past, no hangups, no worries. And Rick . . . well, Rick *is* fucking. He's cock. He's an ice-cream cone with two flavours and jimmies on the top. Sometimes I remember that I'm seventeen and I wonder what it's like to be a little girl again and I think I've lived almost all of my life already, but then I get back into the 'now', and it's alright. I could kill Rick then, those dark times, but they never last.

Blackout.

A light shines on MAGGIE's *face.*

CLAY: Maggie.

MAGGIE: This is foolish. I wouldn't really kill him. I don't have a motive.

CLAY: You're an actress.

JADE: Pretend.

MAGGIE: When did you last see me *act*? Oh, I used to. For years. Off-Broadway, summer stock, road companies, learning my craft, becoming really good. Got me nowhere. One day I looked around and saw what was happening. *Crazy* was happening. So I made myself into a loon. Got invited everywhere. Now I'm no longer an actress. I'm a *star*. I go to openings, closings, funerals, parties, seminars, ballgames, races, marches, meetings, birthdays, weddings, street-fairs, rodeos – as long as there's a camera, or a reporter, to record it. A star! And Rick? Well, baby, the biggest star of us all. He's more than a good lay, you know what I mean? He's good publicity! As soon as I have an orgasm, I phone the papers. You know – I make it into a funny story. The whole fucockta world cares about us. But listen, I'm not dumb. He's tiring of the older woman bit. (*Slightly* older.) He's gonna move on. Well – not now! I'm gonna be The Lady In Black. I'll be up to my ass in flowers, and tears, and urns, and syndicated columns about our last sublime moments together. And if I'm lucky, I can milk it for at least six months. So? How's *that* for a motive?

Blackout.

A light shines on SAMMY's *face.*

CLAY: Sammy.

SAMMY: Sure, I could have killed him. You know when I met Rick? Ten years ago. In a small southern town, the night of a civil rights march. Oh yeah, I was big in civil rights. Honey, I registered *more* voters than the whole Department of Justice. Big favour I did them! Anyhow, Rick was just starting, singing kind of straight then. He had a concert scheduled in town that night. What did he know? Boy, even then he was sexy. Fucked me up. Fucked me up – and down, actually, but that's another story. No, it's not. It's what it's all about. He was mean, physically *mean*. And I dug it. That was the beginning of my disorientation. Afterward, nothing seemed like exactly what it was. Well, civil rights became complicated, weren't no place for a white boy no more, and there were other things to drift into; flowers, honey, I wore flowers in my hair for years, and speed in my brain, and always, at intervals, I'd come back to Rick, and he'd fuck me up and down again, and I'd leave, always more confused than before. You see, Rick made me turn to religion. If I had found Satan so *easily*, why not look for God? Oh, I looked in strange places. Like all good Jewish boys, I became a Buddhist. But that's obscure, very obscure. So I became a Catholic, which is easy, they'll take *anyone*. And one day, while I was floating through France, I came upon this cute town with a divine Benedictine mission. I badgered them for two years and finally they accepted me as a novice. It's their custom – if you're enough of a yenta, they'll accept you. So Tuesday I fly Air France to become a monk. I'm even gonna give up outside fucking. Only do it with other monks. And you know, I'm really into it, into God and things. Now, I know that's a little convoluted, but I think that's reason enough to kill Rick.

Blackout.

A light shines on NADINE's *face.*

CLAY: Nadine.

NADINE: I was a student doing my thesis on 'The Psychology of Rock'. I went to interview Rick, and, well, one thing led to another . . . I guess I never got the interview. After a couple of weeks of travelling with Rick, a paper on the psychology of *anything* seemed absurd, so I left school, and also, I left group therapy, although Cynthia didn't want me to go, Cynthia was my analyst, a nice middle-aged lady . . . Well, I got into a lot of different scenes – communes, ashrams – for a while all I did was milk goats – and then, some heavy relationships and some real bad drugs – lots of changes, I was very loose and not really *motivated*, you know. Then one day I bumped into this kid who had been in my group and he told me that Cynthia had killed herself. A lot of analysts commit suicide these days. It's sort of the logical conclusion of their work. Well, I was very struck by this . . . I guess I felt guilty, maybe if I had stayed in group, I could have helped her. I began thinking about her all the time, and then one day . . . (*Her voice assumes the other tone:*) Don't tell them. (*Her natural tone:*) Oh. That's Cynthia. One day she entered my body. Her spirit, that is. You know – a dybbuk. Well, we've been together ever since, and while it's been difficult, I think, in my way, I've been able to help.

CLAY: How about Rick?

NADINE: Oh, I would never kill him. When I needed help, he gave me money, and he lets me crash in this house. He's really the only person who's been good to me. (*As Cynthia:*) What do you think I've been? (*as herself:*) Lay off it, will you, Cynthia? (*As Cynthia:*) You've always misplaced your affections. (*herself:*) Lay off . . . (*As Cynthia:*) Why can't you see Rick for what he is? He likes to encourage your eccentricities, that's all. He doesn't really care about you. (*herself:*) Stop it! (*As Cynthia:*) I hate the bastard! (*herself:*) I would never kill Rick. *Cynthia* would.

Blackout.

A light shines on GIDEON's *face.*

CLAY: Gideon.

GIDEON: The light's too bright. Turn it down. O.K., man, I know what you're thinking. Jealousy. Poor Gideon playing his guitar two steps out of the spotlight, while Rick stands stage centre, getting all the attention with his jerk-off routines. Poor Gideon. Shit, man, poor Gideon had a *good* time. Good music, good dope, good chicks . . . I loved it, the whole ten-year gig. I didn't want it to end. I'd have to be crazy to kill him. Ah! Maybe *that's* it. Think whatever you want. I don't care.

Blackout.

A light shines on ROBERTA's *face.*

CLAY: Roberta.

ROBERTA: The guy was a creep. Still, he took me in when no one wanted me. Yeah, I had a rough time. All those headlines – 'Teamster Changes Sex!' Ahh, people are pigs, they don't understand. You see, it's not related to sex drives – you got that? It's just biological, I wasn't the gender my body said it was, see, and it got embarrassing, being on the docks, you know, and wearing dresses. But they got this operation now and they fix you up good. I'm much happier, I got to say that, *much* happier. Oh yeah – well, he needed a bodyguard, all those screaming kids at his concerts, trying to get on stage, touch him, pull his clothes apart. He was surrounded by a lot of weirdos, I'll tell you that. I mean, his friends too. Perverts. Made me nervous. Sure, if I got good and mad, I could have totalled him. Why not?

Blackout.

A light shines on IRENE's *face.*

CLAY: Irene.

IRENE: I'd rather not.

CLAY: Go on. Everyone else has.

IRENE: Gosh, I had no reason to kill Rick. I hadn't seen him for years. He's asked me to come visit a lot, but my husband, Barry, doesn't approve of him, so this trip, with Barry away and everything, was my first chance . . . Barry's an army career man and Rick – well, he dances around with rattlesnakes and whips, and sings in falsetto. They're not used to that at Fort Myers. (Why do you think he was painting his whole body like that?) You know, when Rick was on stage, he didn't make any sense, not to me. I always want things to be logical. But just because he wasn't Andy Williams is no reason to kill him. I'm sorry. I don't have a motive.

CLAY: You grew up with him. There has to be something.

IRENE: Oh – well – we were kids together, you know how kids are. What do you want me to tell you, that he pulled my braids? Sure, he pulled my braids. And in the third grade he used to report me all the time to Miss Lane for talking; Miss Lane was deaf; she

didn't know *who* was talking; I always had to stay after school. And if that's a motive, you're welcome to it.

Blackout.

CLAY (*in darkness*): Someone take the camera.

A light shines on CLAY's *face.*
SAMMY *holds the camera and lights.*

SAMMY: Clay.

CLAY: I used to be Rick's lawyer. Drug busts, paternity suits, indecent exposure . . . the usual stuff. I was a very *good* lawyer. I won a famous case before the Supreme Court. The Bruno Decision. It meant that policemen had to show their badge number at the exact moment of arrest. My wife was especially proud of me; she believed in just causes. She was Navajo. I took her away from her reservation, away from the clear sky, into the city. One night, coming home from a concert, she was robbed and raped and stabbed. She died five days later. They caught the guy. A junkie. He went on trial, but he got off on a technicality. The policeman had neglected to show his badge number at the exact moment of arrest. The Bruno Decision. I lost interest in law. I was pretty low. That was the first time I took acid. While I was tripping, I heard a voice, very clearly, saying, 'Clay, you should get into pornography.' So I bought a movie camera and got some friends together . . . Now I make the biggest grossing adult films in the country. What the hell. (*Pause.*) Oh yes – Rick. Rick owns fifty per cent of my film company. Now I can have it all.

Blackout.

Scene Four

The lights rise on the house. CLAY *is putting the camera down, and dismantling the lights, aided by* SAMMY. NADINE *is in the study, sitting next to* RICK's *body.* GIDEON *is smoking a joint,* MAGGIE *pacing,* JADE *sitting in a yoga position,* ROBERTA *guarding the garden doors.* IRENE *walks to the telephone.*

IRENE: I think we should try the police again.

NADINE (*staring at* RICK): He looks so sad.

GIDEON *takes the telephone, tries it.*

GIDEON: The lines are still dead.

ROBERTA: Someone cut them, huh?

GIDEON: It was just the tremor. It often happens.

SAMMY: If there's a police station nearby, I can drive over . . .

ROBERTA: Nobody leaves the house! One of you jerks is a killer.

IRENE: That's ridiculous. There were at least twenty other people at the party.

MAGGIE: Oh God! I forgot about them! I really thought it was one of us. Maybe even me. Is the egg-nog still in the garden? (*Goes to garden door.*)

ROBERTA: I said nobody leaves.

MAGGIE: Relax. I'm just going a few feet. (ROBERTA *lets her pass.* MAGGIE *goes into the garden.* IRENE *walks into the study.*)

SAMMY: I think we should make a list of the people at the party, before we all forget.

CLAY: It does make sense that the killer would leave. That's a shame. I got such nice motives on film. Oh well – (*Takes a bunch of writing pads from a coffee table and gives one each to* GIDEON, JADE *and* ROBERTA.) Write down who you remember.

IRENE (*looking at* RICK's *body*): I hardly knew him. I never had a brother. He was *like* a brother. That was a long time ago. We all grow up and lose each other. It's a shame.

NADINE: Maybe we should cover him.

IRENE: I'll get a sheet.

NADINE: No. A blanket. Something pretty.

IRENE *leaves the study and walks up the stairs, to the second floor.* MAGGIE *returns to the living room with a large bowl of egg nog. She puts the bowl on a table and pours herself a cup. The others are absorbed, trying to remember names, occasionally writing on their pads.*

GIDEON (*looks up*): Do you remember who that bearded cat was?

JADE: Brown hair?

GIDEON: Yeah.

JADE: Oleg. He's Russian. You know what he told me? He said he fucked his cat, and he's worried that the cat is pregnant. I think he shoots up, though, so it may not be true.

MAGGIE: Put his name at the top of the list, with a star by it!

SAMMY *puts his pad down, and walks into the study.* MAGGIE *picks up* SAMMY's *pad and starts to write a name.* NADINE *is singing a lullaby, softly, to* RICK, SAMMY *watches her.*

SAMMY: Don't you think we should leave him alone?

NADINE: No. I'm his friend. The others aren't. Except maybe you.

SAMMY: Yeah. Maybe. It's awful. I want to touch his body. I want to make love to him right now. Do you think that's the worst thought I'll ever have?

NADINE: I think it's beautiful. I think you should.

SAMMY: Look, there's blood on his neck.

NADINE: He was starting a song that way. He told me about it.

SAMMY: Oh. Right. His act. I forget about his act.

NADINE (*as Cynthia*): It was all an act. (*herself:*) Please leave us alone, Cynthia. Just this once. (*as Cynthia:*) I don't like it here.

SAMMY: Maybe she's afraid.

NADINE: Of what?

SAMMY: Another dead spirit.

MAGGIE *looks up from her pad.*

MAGGIE: There's that dwarf who used to be with the Peace Corps and now she's an embalmer . . .

GIDEON: Harriet Perlow.

MAGGIE: Right. (MAGGIE *writes it down.*)

NADINE: Can't you do something religious over him?

SAMMY: I haven't learned how yet.

CLAY *looks up from his pad.*

CLAY: How about that young man with the live goldfish in his earring? Who was he?

JADE: Oh wow. He was weird. He showed me his scar. (JADE *goes back to her pad. The others look at her.*)

MAGGIE: And? . . .

JADE: Oh, nothing. It was very big. He used to weigh two hundred and fifty pounds, but he had this operation and they cut miles and miles of intestines out of him and so now he's thin and handsome and really ready to cat around, you see, except that he suddenly has this strange compulsion to only sleep with very fat women, which he doesn't understand, but there it is, so that's why he wouldn't go to bed with me. (*She returns to her pad. A silence.*)

MAGGIE: Oh.

GIDEON: Well, did he have a name?

JADE (*looks up*): I guess.

MAGGIE: We should crack this case in no time.

IRENE *returns down the stairs, carrying a blanket. She takes it into the study.*

NADINE (*as Cynthia*): Please, Nadine. (*herself:*) In a little while.

IRENE: I found this. It's colourful. (*Starts to drape it over* RICK.)

SAMMY: Don't! (SAMMY *bends down, touches* RICK's *face, then turns away.*)

IRENE *covers the body.*

NADINE (*softly*): Goodbye, Rick. (NADINE *rises and walks into the living room.* IRENE *looks at* RICK's *body, then the doorway into the living room. She points to the door.*)

IRENE: It had to be this way.

SAMMY: What?

IRENE: The bullet. The gun. From this direction.

SAMMY: It could have come from the window.

IRENE: Not the way he was hit. The killer had to be standing in the doorway. Oh, here I go, always trying to *solve* everything. I should leave it to the police. (IRENE *and* SAMMY *walk into the living room.* MAGGIE *puts down her pad.*)

MAGGIE: I'm sorry, I don't remember anyone else.

GIDEON: Yeah. This is it for me.

CLAY *takes their pads, and then collects the pads from* ROBERTA *and* JADE.

CLAY: About nine names between us . . .

GIDEON: He'll be miles away by now.

ROBERTA: Unless he's right here in this room.

MAGGIE (*goes to* ROBERTA *and offers him a cup*): Listen, have some egg-nog. It will help you relax.

ROBERTA: They're gonna think it's me.

MAGGIE: What do you mean?

ROBERTA: Nothing. But I didn't do it.

MAGGIE: Nobody here did it.

ROBERTA: How do you know?

CLAY (*to* JADE): I'd like to photograph the study. Would you like to help? (*Picks up his camera.*)

JADE.: I don't want to go into that room again. (*to* GIDEON:) Do you have some dope?

GIDEON: Sure. (*Hands* JADE *a joint.*)

JADE (*lighting it*): It's not right in that room. It's all past, you know what I mean? Rick is no longer in the 'now'.

MAGGIE: Guess that says it as well as anything. (GIDEON *offers her a joint.*) No thanks. The egg-nog's all whisky. Well, I suppose I'm a free lady now. Are you interested?

GIDEON: Hey, his body's still warm.

MAGGIE: So is mine. Ahh, I'm kidding. Don't let it get you.

GIDEON: Sit down.

MAGGIE: I'm nervous. I want to pace. (*Sits.*) There. Are you upset? You really liked him, huh?

GIDEON: I guess. Liked him, didn't like

him at all, loved him, you know? I just can't figure out what's going to happen *now*. Forget it. You're not too upset.

MAGGIE: Do you know how many guys have left me? A lot. Of course, I've never had one get shot before.

CLAY *walks to the door between the living room and the study.* IRENE *is there, looking at the door.* JADE *walks up to* CLAY.

JADE: I don't think we should go into that room anymore. Not unless we put the body on a pyre and burn it . . . They do that in India, and they seem to know best. (*Wanders off again.*)

CLAY (*to* IRENE): You're sure the bullet came from here?

IRENE: Fairly sure.

CLAY: Wonder why we didn't hear anything.

IRENE: There was so much noise in the garden.

CLAY: I guess. And then the killer walked calmly back into the party . . . Perhaps we should look for the gun.

IRENE: Why?

CLAY: Well, if it were a man, he'd have a problem. Everything's so skin-tight these days. There's no place to hide a gun.

IRENE: So maybe it was a woman.

CLAY: I don't know. (*Takes her hand.*) You're very pretty. You're the type I never get into my films.

IRENE (*pulls her hand away*): Gosh. Is that an offer?

Suddenly, the lights flicker and dim, then go out. It is dark. Completely dark. Nothing can be seen.

SAMMY: Now what?

IRENE: Oh dear, is it another earthquake?

MAGGIE: Nothing's moving.

CLAY: This happens sometimes after a tremor. A delayed power-failure.

IRENE: What a city!

JADE: It's very sexy like this. Who am I next to?

ROBERTA: Hands off, creep.

NADINE (*as Cynthia*): Let's get out of here. Please.

MAGGIE: Who was that? I didn't recognize that voice. There's a stranger in this room.

NADINE: That was Cynthia.

MAGGIE: Oh, her.

GIDEON: Hey, you're really jumpy.

MAGGIE: Yeah. Well, why not? It's goddamn dark in here, and there's a dead body in the next room . . .

GIDEON: Calm down, calm down . . .

IRENE: Aren't there any candles?

SAMMY: Uh-huh. There's a life size candle upstairs, sculpted in Rick's image, but I'm not into lighting *that*.

MAGGIE: I think I heard a bat.

GIDEON: That's ridiculous.

JADE: Maybe we should all meditate.

NADINE: There were lots of candles in the garden.

CLAY: Where's my camera?

IRENE: You just had it.

CLAY: But I put it down. I can't find it.

GIDEON: No one's going to steal your camera.

IRENE: Why don't we get the candles from the garden?

ROBERTA: Nobody leaves this room!

NADINE (*as Cynthia*): Now Roberta, if we *all* go to the garden we can each take a candle; that way, we will *all* be together and then we will *all* have a lot of light.

MAGGIE: Was that Cynthia?

NADINE: Yes.

MAGGIE: Just checking. She sounded like an analyst, didn't she?

JADE: If we meditate, we'll have an *inner* light.

CLAY: I know I put the camera somewhere. What's this?

ROBERTA: Hands off, creep.

CLAY: Sorry.

MAGGIE (*an ungodly screech*): HOLD IT! DON'T MOVE!

SAMMY: What is it?

GIDEON: What happened?

MAGGIE: My contact lens slipped out.

SAMMY: Jesus!

MAGGIE: I have it! It's on my finger.

IRENE: You scared me half to death.

MAGGIE: O.K. Which way to the garden?

GIDEON: Come on. Take my hand. Here.

SAMMY: Whose hand is this?

GIDEON: I guess it's mine.

SAMMY: That's fine with me.

MAGGIE: I have somebody's hand. Is it yours?

NADINE: It's mine.

MAGGIE: Cynthia?

NADINE: Nadine.

GIDEON: We can just feel our way to the door . . .

JADE: This is fun.

SAMMY: I have the door. Come on . . .

ROBERTA: Nobody try any tricks . . .

SAMMY: This way . . .

Slowly, hand in hand, they all feel their way into the garden, except for CLAY, *who is still searching for his camera.*

CLAY: It's amazing. I'm such a well-ordered person, and then I lose everything. I was sure the camera was right here. Irene? Are you still here? If I find the camera, maybe you'll really think about it, about doing a little film for me. Irene? She isn't here. Is *anybody* here? Maybe she'll do a little film for me . . . What's this? A typewriter? I must be in the study. The camera's in the living room. She's very attractive. I'd like to see her breasts. I'd like to film her in bed with someone. As long as I have my camera . . . How could I lose it? You just don't lose something like that, it doesn't make any sense . . .

A shot rings out.

There is a long silence.

Voices are heard in the garden.

MAGGIE (*off, in the garden*): What was it?

GIDEON (*off, in the garden*): Stay here.

GIDEON *enters, holding a burning candle. He moves the candle around the living room.* MAGGIE *enters, followed by* IRENE *and* SAMMY. *They are also holding burning candles.*

GIDEON: Don't come in.

SAMMY: It's empty.

MAGGIE: Well, it *sounded* like a shot.

JADE *and* NADINE *enter, followed by* ROBERTA. *They also hold burning candles.*

SAMMY (*points to study*): Do you think?

JADE: Don't go in there.

GIDEON, SAMMY, MAGGIE *and* IRENE *enter the study.* GIDEON *moves his candle around.* ROBERTA *and* NADINE *join them.* JADE *stays in the living room.* GIDEON's *candle throws a light on* CLAY's *body.* CLAY *is lying on the floor, dead.*

IRENE: Oh dear Lord.

NADINE: Is he dead?

GIDEON (*bends over body*): Yes.

MAGGIE: So much for the guest list.

IRENE: I guess it's one of us.

Blackout.

Curtain.

ACT TWO

Scene One

A half hour later.

The house is ablaze with candles of all shapes and sizes, bathing the living room and study in an eerie light. A fire burns in the fireplace.

CLAY's body has been covered with a blanket. It remains on the floor of the study, near RICK's body.

NADINE is sitting at a table, playing Monopoly with Cynthia.

GIDEON, JADE and MAGGIE are on the floor. GIDEON has a tray in front of him; there is some white powder on the tray, arranged in three sections. He takes a rolled up dollar bill, and sniffs one section of powder. JADE and MAGGIE are awaiting their turn.

IRENE sits in the study. She is staring at the two bodies and is deep in thought.

ROBERTA is outside, in the garden, with his back against the garden door, either protecting or imprisoning the people inside.

SAMMY comes down the stairway, carrying a huge candelabra.

MAGGIE: Enough candles, already. The house is gonna burn down.

SAMMY: This is the last. I promise. (*Takes the candelabra into the study.*)

GIDEON: Beautiful! (*Dreamily passes the cocaine and the dollar bill to JADE.*)

SAMMY (*in the study – to* IRENE): Where shall I put this?

IRENE: What?

SAMMY: The candelabra.

IRENE: I don't know. Anywhere. Did you check the cars?

SAMMY: There's no way to get to them. A tree is down in front of the garage.

IRENE: Can't we walk?

SAMMY: Down the canyon road?

IRENE: Sure.

SAMMY: It can take us hours, and even then we might not find a cop. The phone's are never out for long. Relax.

IRENE: It's all so confusing.

SAMMY: What is?

IRENE (*points to* RICK *and* CLAY): This.

SAMMY: Try not to think about it. (*Puts the candelabra on the desk.*)

IRENE: We were *all* in the garden, weren't we?

SAMMY (*lighting candles*): Who knows? It was dark. I don't know where *you* were for sure. Do you know exactly where I was?

IRENE: I guess not. But aren't you worried?

SAMMY: You mean that one of us is bonkers? Listen, I've been around so many nuts, I figure my life is almost always in danger. Last week, this bum, very drunk, wobbled up to me in the street and said, 'Hey, mister, if I had a gun, I'd kill you' and I looked at him, and realized, sure 'nuff, if he *had* had a gun, he'd have killed me. Once a week, honey, once a week, you come across someone like that. So there's a lunatic running amok in this house? What can you do?

IRENE: But there might be clues. Maybe we can figure out who it is.

SAMMY: Well – I figure 'who can figure?' Of course, now that I'm Catholic, I have some security. *We* get to go to Heaven. If I were still Jewish, maybe I'd worry.

SAMMY goes into the living room.

JADE has snorted the cocaine. She hands the tray to MAGGIE.

MAGGIE: You know, all the parties I've been to, and I've never done this before. I always pass it by. (GIDEON *and* JADE *look at her.*) You don't want to give me any hints? (GIDEON *and* JADE *are, at the moment, too high to talk.*) If I don't like it, can I keep the dollar bill? (*Puts her hand against one nostril.*) Here goes . . . (*Sniffs some powder. A pause.*) I like it better in bottles.

SAMMY sits down next to MAGGIE.

SAMMY: Is there any left? (MAGGIE

shakes her head no.) What a drag. I
don't think they'll offer me any coke at
the monastery, not for a while, not until
they're sure I'm cool. How y'doing?
(MAGGIE *just stares at him.*) You're
doin' alright. (*Lights a joint.*)

ROBERTA *comes in from the garden
and looks around.*

ROBERTA: Now, nobody try a run for
the door, you hear me? (*The others
ignore him.* NADINE *is moving her
player-piece on the Monopoly board,
and counting the steps as she moves.*)

NADINE: One, two, three, four . . . shit.
(*as Cynthia:*) New Hampshire! That's
mine. Four hundred dollars. (*herself:*)
You're just lucky. (NADINE *gives
herself four hundred dollars.*
ROBERTA *goes to* NADINE, *and
moves a chair beside her. He is
drinking egg-nog.*)

ROBERTA: Hey, listen, lady, can I sit?

NADINE: Sure.

ROBERTA: I been watching you. I don't
think you're the one.

NADINE (*smiles*): Oh, you can't be too
sure.

ROBERTA: Hey, don't get me wrong. I
don't mean you're not crazy, you're
plenty crazy, but I don't think you're a
killer. The others – it's written all over
them, you gotta watch them like a
hawk.

NADINE: I will.

IRENE: Listen, lady, can I ask you a
favour?

NADINE: Sure.

IRENE: When the police come, they'll
arrest me.

NADINE (*as Cynthia*): Why do you say
that?

IRENE: Huh? Oh, it's that voice trick of
yours. Yeah, well, see, I'm easy to pick
on.

NADINE (*as Cynthia*): What makes you
think that?

IRENE: It's just the way it is.

NADINE (*as Cynthia, very much the
analyst*): You must have reasons. Try
to remember.

IRENE: Well, you're working on the
dock, unloading bananas, you know,
and the guys, they throw things down
your bra, and when a shipment's
missing, they say it's you, that you
need the money for a new pair of
stocking; you're just a target, that's all.

NADINE (*as Cynthia*): How long have
you had these feelings? (*herself:*)
Cynthia, don't! (*to* ROBERTA:)
What's the favour?

ROBERTA: Call this number for me. My
wife. Let her know before the papers
get to her. (*Hands* NADINE *a slip of
paper.*)

NADINE: O.K. (*as Cynthia:*) You didn't
say you had a wife.

ROBERTA: Yeah. I do.

NADINE (*as Cynthia*): What are your
feelings about her?

ROBERTA: I love her, what d'you think?
I mean, she's been very understanding,
very understanding.

NADINE (*as Cynthia*): Do you still
maintain relations with her?

ROBERTA: What kind?

NADINE (*as Cynthia*): Sexual.

ROBERTA: Hey, lady, what do you think
I am, some kind of lesbo?

MAGGIE *has wandered over to them
during the last part of the
conversation. She pulls a chair over
and sits down. She is very stoned.*

MAGGIE: You know, I tried to be a
lesbian for a whole year. Really worked
at it. But it didn't take. It's a shame
because men have so many problems
. . . (*to* ROBERTA:) You're well out of
it. Believe me. It's a fucking *smart*
choice.

ROBERTA: Don't talk dirty to me.

SAMMY *walks over to them.*

MAGGIE: Oh. Sorry. My second
husband liked me to talk dirty. He was
like a little boy. I don't get it – what's
so great about being a little boy again?

SAMMY: Well, honey, it wasn't much fun
the first time around, so we're just
trying to get it right. (*Pulls over a chair
and sits down.*)

NADINE (*as Cynthia, to* SAMMY): Did you have a difficult childhood?

SAMMY: Of course. Didn't you?

NADINE (*as Cynthia*): We're not discussing my childhood.

SAMMY: We're not discussing *my* childhood either. What is this?

NADINE (*as Cynthia*): Why are you resisting me?

SAMMY: What are you going on about?

MAGGIE: You know something, you *are* resisting her. What are you hiding?

ROBERTA: Maybe you should tell!

NADINE: Oh God, Cynthia, you have a *group* going!

IRENE *walks into the living room from the study. She is very excited.*

IRENE: Something's on the tape! (*The others look up, startled.*)

SAMMY: What?

IRENE: Something's on the tapes he made! Something that gives it away. That's why he was killed.

GIDEON: Who was killed?

IRENE: Clay. (*The others just stare at her.*) There are two dead bodies in there. Doesn't anyone care?

SAMMY: What was on the tapes?

IRENE: I *don't* know. That's just it. But it's the logical reason for his being murdered. When he would show the tapes, he'd discover the identity of Rick's killer. So the killer had to get Clay first, don't you see?

MAGGIE: I did an Agatha Christie play once, and I didn't understand a word of it.

IRENE: I'm *very* serious.

SAMMY: Oh, honey, it just doesn't pay.

NADINE (*as Cynthia*): Why do you have a *need* to be serious?

IRENE: You're *all* crazy.

ROBERTA: Watch it, lady!

IRENE: Shouldn't we try to look at the tapes?

GIDEON (*gets up, still dreamy*): Oh, man, it's over anyway. It's all over.

What's the use (*Pulls* JADE *up.*) Come here . . . (GIDEON *takes* JADE *to the fireplace. They sit in front of the fire.* IRENE *walks to the garden door and stands looking into the garden.* GIDEON *is holding* JADE's *hand.*)

GIDEON: Can you understand what I'm trying to tell you? It's no more. Man, they were the best days of my life. You know what it was like up until then? How could you know? When were you born? Ahh, you missed it, you were born too late. You missed all those boring years when nothing happened and everyone looked the same. Do you know how ugly I was? Oh yeah, it's true. I mean, it's not true, I wasn't ugly at all, but people thought I was, because I looked strange, exotic, freaky, you know, not like anyone else. Kids used to laugh at me in the streets and they were right, my clothes never fit, you try to be skinny back then, they didn't make clothes for you, no one was skinny. But suddenly overnight, the world changed, and *all* the clothes were being made for you, and strange was fine, and freaky became a compliment, and I was beautiful, and the same kids in the street pointed to me and waved and said oh wow; and my mind, too, my *mind* suddenly made sense; off-centre was centre, or there was no centre or *something*, but it all fit in. I fit in. And being with Rick's band, sure, that made sense, I was an *asset* – oh yeah, those were good days . . . But it's all speeding up, speeding up and slowing down at the same time, and I don't think I understand it anymore, and if Rick's dead, the times are dead, and what's going to happen to me? Do you think I'll become ugly again? Am I going to have to change? I like it the way I am! Oh, man, you're so spaced out . . . do you know what I'm saying? (JADE *stares at him for a moment in silence.*)

JADE: This girl I know. She's twenty two. She said when she was my age she was making plaster casts of guys' cocks. She said it was better then – in the old days . . .

GIDEON: Yeah. Like that kind of thing doesn't happen anymore. I mean, that's six years old. A lifetime.

JADE: Want me to do it?

GIDEON: What?

JADE: Make a plaster cast of your cock. Then maybe you'll know it's alright, what was then can still live in the 'now'. Oh yes. Let me do it. Rick has some plaster in his game room. I'll mix it, then you come upstairs and I'll go down on you and get you real hard and we'll put you in the cast, and you won't be unhappy anymore. Oh yes. Let me do it. Please.

GIDEON: Do you think you can?

JADE (*stands up*): I'm getting the plaster. I'll call you when it's ready. (JADE *goes upstairs.*)

IRENE *turns around, once again excited.*

IRENE: Also – Clay was a lawyer! You forget that! He handled all of Rick's legal work. That included Rick's will, and heaven knows what else, and so he knew better than anyone who had the most to gain from Rick's death, and who had the most reason to shut him up. (*The others look at her.*) Oh, for Pete's sake, don't you *care*? (*Disgusted, she turns back and stares at the garden.*)

NADINE (*as Cynthia*): I believe Sammy was telling us about his childhood.

SAMMY: I most certainly was not.

NADINE (*as Cynthia*): Is your hostility based on the fact that I'm a woman?

SAMMY: I'm not hostile.

NADINE: He really *isn't*, Cynthia. Can't we go back to Monopoly? (*as Cynthia:*) Why are you defending him? Why are you angry at me?

SAMMY: She's not angry at you.

NADINE (*as Cynthia*): Why are *you* defending *her*? Is this a conspiracy? (*herself:*) There's no conspiracy. (*as Cynthia:*) What do you have against me?

ROBERTA: Hey, lady, don't get upset.

NADINE (*to* ROBERTA): Leave her alone. (*as Cynthia:*) This man is trying to comfort me.

ROBERTA: I ain't a man no more.

NADINE (*as Cynthia*): Well, I can't help that. You should have come to me sooner.

ROBERTA: What's she talking about?

SAMMY: Don't pay any mind.

NADINE (*as Cynthia, to* SAMMY): You hate me. You hate your mother. You hate Marilyn Monroe.

SAMMY: I *loved* Marilyn Monroe.

NADINE (*as Cynthia*): Because she was a *parody* of woman, that's why! She wasn't real!

MAGGIE: What was wrong with Marilyn Monroe?

NADINE (*as Cynthia, crying*): I tried to help, all my life I tried to help . . . but suddenly no one would listen. (*herself:*) It's all right, Cynthia, it's all right. Don't get upset. Please.

A loud bell rings in the study.

IRENE: What's that? (*She runs into the study.*)

ROBERTA: Burglar alarm?

IRENE (*walks out of study holding an alarm clock*): It's only a clock. (*Turns the alarm off.*) Actually, it's Rick's clock. Why do you think he set it for two twenty-three?

SAMMY (*joking*): Maybe it's a clue.

IRENE: Well, anything could be a clue.

SAMMY: You mean there's a message there in the time? Two twenty-three?

GIDEON: But only *that* clock says two twenty-three. How about the others?

SAMMY: What others?

GIDEON: There's a clock in every room upstairs.

MAGGIE (*standing up*): Then there are lots of clues.

IRENE: You're making fun of me.

MAGGIE: Let's get them. We can compare all the clocks, see what time they're set for, and find out who dun it. Come on.

IRENE: This is really very serious.

MAGGIE: Come on. We'll take a room apiece. (MAGGIE *starts up the stairs.* SAMMY *and* GIDEON *follow her.*)

ROBERTA: Hey – don't try any funny

stuff! (ROBERTA *goes up the stairs after the others.*)

IRENE: I'm very serious. (*She turns, opens the garden door, and leaves – into the garden. There is a silence.*)

NADINE (*as Cynthia*): Nadine? (*herself:*) What? (*as Cynthia:*) I'm sorry. (*silence*) (*herself:*) I told you. (*as Cynthia:*) I know. (*herself:*) You can't go back to that. (*as Cynthia:*) I know. (*herself:*) That's all over. (*as Cynthia:*) I know. (*silence*) (*herself:*) You're safe here. Safe with me. I'm always going to take care of you. No one's ever going to hurt you again. I won't let them. You're never going to leave me. Are you? Please, don't leave me. It's awful . . . alone. Cynthia? (*as Cynthia:*) What? (*herself:*) Please . . . (*as Cynthia:*) I won't leave. I promise. (*silence*) (*herself:*) This house isn't good anymore. (*as Cynthia:*) Ghosts. (*herself:*) What? (*as Cynthia:*) It has ghosts. They want to talk to me. (*herself:*) Should we go? (*as Cynthia:*) Yes. Now. (*herself:*) Cynthia, did . . . (*as Cynthia:*) What? (*herself:*) Nothing. (*as Cynthia:*) Say it. (*herself:*) No. (*as Cynthia:*) We have no secrets. (*herself:*) Don't we? (*as Cynthia:*) What do you mean? (*herself:*) You hated Rick. (*as Cynthia:*) That was hardly a secret. (*herself:*) Then did you . . . did you kill him? (*silence*) (*herself:*) Oh, Cynthia, was it you? I'm praying, praying that it wasn't. Tell me the truth. Did you kill Rick? (*as Cynthia:*) No. I didn't. (*herself:*) Then who did? You know, don't you? (*as Cynthia:*) No. (*herself:*) Oh yes, you do . . . (*as Cynthia:*) Can't we leave here now? (*herself:*) Spirits talk to you. (*as Cynthia:*) No. (*herself:*) Tell me . . . (*as Cynthia:*) It's only a possibility. (*herself:*) A possibility? (*as Cynthia:*) A thought . . . (*herself:*) Well, what is it? (as Cynthia:) You won't believe me. (*herself:*) I will. (*as Cynthia:*) No. You won't. (*herself:*) I'll try. Please Cynthia. It's important. *Tell* me. (*as Cynthia:*) Alright. I think it's . . . (*A shot rings out. NADINE gasps. Her eyes bulge wide open . . . Another shot rings out. NADINE [and Cynthia] falls over the Monopoly board, dead. Silence.*)

IRENE *runs in from the garden.*
MAGGIE, SAMMY, GIDEON *and* ROBERTA *come down the stairs. They each hold an alarm clock. They all stare at NADINE. Suddenly, the lights come on again, full blast. It is very bright. They look at each other.*

Silence.

JADE *comes to the top of the stairs. She appears to be unaware of what's happening.*

JADE: The plaster's ready. (GIDEON *continues to look at* NADINE. *He appears to be so stoned that he can't take it all in.*)

JADE: Gideon! (GIDEON *backs away from* NADINE's *body, and walks backward, up the stairs, his hand reaching out for* JADE. *She takes his hand, and they go off.*)

MAGGIE *walks to the sofa. She sits. She looks at her clock.*

MAGGIE: Mine says four-thirty. (*She drops the clock on the sofa.*)

SAMMY *kneels by* NADINE's *body.*

SAMMY: I should have told her about my childhood. What did I have to lose? It would have made her happy. I should have dredged up some old memories for her. (*Sings, softly:*)
  'Oh today we'll merry merry be
  Oh today we'll merry merry be
  Oh today we'll merry merry be
  And have some homintashin.'
We used to sing that at Purim. When I was a kid, Purim was my favourite holiday. I should have told her that. She wanted to help.

MAGGIE: I remember that song. I was thirteen and I dressed up as Queen Esther and won second prize in the Hebrew School costume parade. That was the start of my career. (*Sings, with spirit:*)
  'Oh today we'll merry merry be
  Oh today we'll merry merry be . . .
(SAMMY *joins her.*)

MAGGIE and SAMMY:
  'Oh today we'll merry merry be
  And have some homintashin.'

Silence.

IRENE: What's homintashin? Oh, for heavens sake, listen to me! I don't care about *that*. (*Points to* NADINE.) I care about this.

SAMMY (*softly*): So do I. (*Looks up.*) Are there more blankets upstairs? (SAMMY *walks up the stairs to the second floor.*)

ROBERTA (*looking at* NADINE): She was alright. (*To the others:*) I warned her about you guys.

IRENE: Well maybe now we can all start to seriously worry.

MAGGIE: I don't feel too well.

IRENE: She knew. Of course! She had to know who the killer was. That's why she was shot. I mean, she understood human behaviour, she was an analyst. That is, she thought she was an analyst. Gosh, it gets confusing. (*Looks around.*) And she was shot from there – from that window. (*Points to window next to the stairs.*) That would seem to be the right angle, don't you think?

Silence.

MAGGIE: Who knows?

IRENE: Well just look.

MAGGIE: I don't want to look.

IRENE: And there's a veranda right below the window.

MAGGIE (*Turns around*): But we were all upstairs.

ROBERTA (*to* IRENE): Yeah, except you, *you* were in the garden. (*To* MAGGIE:) You make a note of that. She was in the garden, right next to the veranda.

IRENE: You can reach the veranda just as easily from any of the upstairs windows. It could have been any one of us, including you.

ROBERTA: You watch your step, lady. You're not going to pin this on me.

IRENE: I'm just pointing out that any one of us could have been the killer.

MAGGIE: The rate things are going, I hope it's me.

ROBERTA: Yeah? Maybe it is.

MAGGIE: Now what's *that* mean?

ROBERTA: Just letting you know that I have my eyes open.

MAGGIE: Wonderful.

IRENE (*looking up at the restored lights*): Do you think the phone's back?

MAGGIE (*gets up, goes to the phone*): Let me try. I need some activity. (*Holds the receiver up.*) Nothing.

IRENE: Well, it's silly to just stay here. I can go and get help. Maybe I can get a ride down the road.

MAGGIE: Sure, walk out the front door and never be seen again! We don't play it that way, darling. We can *all* go to the police.

IRENE: Good. *That* makes sense. Let's do it. Where's Sammy?

SAMMY (*coming down the stairs, holding a blanket*): Right here.

MAGGIE: And Gideon?

SAMMY: Upstairs. Getting a blow job.

MAGGIE: Well this is no time for *that*.

SAMMY: Fine. Tell it to him.

IRENE: But it's a matter of life and death.

SAMMY: Honey, sometimes getting a blow-job is a matter of life and death.

IRENE: But *this* is serious.

SAMMY: You keep saying that. *Nothing* is serious. (*Puts blanket over* NADINE*'s body.*) Nothing.

MAGGIE: How long is Gideon going to be?

SAMMY (*looks up*): I'm supposed to answer *that*?

IRENE: We've got to go to the police.

ROBERTA: Not me, lady. I ain't walking in no police station. They'll never let me out.

MAGGIE: We're certainly not going to leave you here alone!

SAMMY (*to* IRENE): So – see? – you're back where you started. So why even start? Relax, honey, everything works out for the best.

JADE *comes to the top of the stairs. She is trembling and crying.*

JADE: Help!

IRENE: Oh no.

JADE: Help. Please . . . somebody come and help . . .

MAGGIE: Gideon!

JADE: I didn't mean for it to happen . . .

MAGGIE: Is he . . .?

JADE: Yes. Stuck.

MAGGIE: *What*?

JADE: He's stuck in the plaster. (SAMMY *starts to laugh.*) I can't get it off. I can't get it out. He's stuck. I don't know what to do.

SAMMY (*still laughing*): I'll take a look. (SAMMY *runs up the stairs. JADE comes down into the living room. IRENE turns to MAGGIE.*)

IRENE: Everything has a pattern. If we can find a pattern, maybe we can figure out who did it.

JADE: I did it. I sucked his cock and put the plaster over it and it got stuck.

IRENE: Darn it, that's *not* what I mean!

SAMMY *comes down the stairs.*

SAMMY: He's stuck alright.

JADE: How do we get it off?

SAMMY: Beats me. It's *not* unattractive.

IRENE (*to* MAGGIE): And then there's the gun. Do you think that one of us is really wearing a gun at this very minute. I doubt it. There *has* to be a hiding place. The sensible thing to do would be to search the entire house, top to bottom . . .

GIDEON *appears at the top of the staircase, naked, except for a plaster cast clinging to his erect penis.*

GIDEON: Oh man, this is grim. (*He comes down the stairs.*)

IRENE: Good heavens!

JADE: My girlfriend never mentioned anything like this happening, but she's been into mescaline pretty heavy and only remembers things in flashes . . .

GIDEON (*going to* MAGGIE *for comfort*): Maggie.

MAGGIE: *Now* you come to me. It's too late.

GIDEON: Rick had *his* done six years ago and nothing went wrong. What will I do?

SAMMY: Won't it get loose if you get soft?

GIDEON: Maybe. But the plaster is stimulating.

ROBERTA: I can take care of it. Just wait a minute. (ROBERTA *rushes up the stairs.*)

MAGGIE (*very bemused*): Can't we just *pull* it off? (GIDEON *glares at her.*) No, huh?

GIDEON (*to* JADE): I tried telling you – it's all over. The good times are gone.

JADE: I don't think you should blame me.

GIDEON: Well – look at it.

JADE: I just wanted to make you happy. I mean, I can do that, *in my way*. (*Stares at* GIDEON.) I'm glad I'm not old.

ROBERTA *comes down the stairs, holding an axe.*

ROBERTA: O.K. This will do it. (*Holds up the axe.*)

SAMMY: Jesus!

ROBERTA (*going to* GIDEON): I'll crack it open.

GIDEON (*backing away from him*): Sure you will!

ROBERTA: Listen, punk, I'm trying to help.

GIDEON: Stay away from me.

ROBERTA: It won't hurt any.

GIDEON: Just keep your distance.

ROBERTA (*going toward him*): I'll have it off in no time flat.

GIDEON: He's *crazy*! (GIDEON *runs into the garden.*)

MAGGIE: Roberta, put that thing down!

ROBERTA: I know what I'm doing. (ROBERTA *goes into the garden.*)

MAGGIE: I'll bet he does.

SAMMY: Roberta! (MAGGIE *and* SAMMY *go after* ROBERTA, *into the garden.*)

IRENE: I don't understand it. Three people are lying dead and you're all playing games.

JADE: Oh it's fun to play games.

GIDEON *runs in from the garden.*

GIDEON: Somebody's got to stop him.

JADE: I think we're supposed to call him 'her'.

ROBERTA *runs in, wielding his axe.*

GIDEON: Stay away! (GIDEON *runs up the stairs.*)

ROBERTA: Hey, come back. This is for your own good ... (ROBERTA *runs up the stairs after* GIDEON. MAGGIE *and* SAMMY *run in from the garden.*)

SAMMY: Roberta, since when have you gotten helpful? (SAMMY *runs upstairs after* ROBERTA.)

MAGGIE (*to* IRENE *and* JADE): Some night, huh? (MAGGIE *follows* SAMMY *up the stairs.*)

IRENE: Look, I'm getting out of here. I'm going to find a police station and bring back some help. You can tell the others for me. (*Gets her handbag from a chair.*)

SAMMY (*upstairs*): Roberta, where are you?

MAGGIE (*upstairs*): Gideon?

IRENE *walks out into the garden.*

JADE: Oh, look at all the clocks. (*Picks up a clock.*) My father used to collect alarm clocks. I don't know why people collect things. It's silly to have possessions. You never know where you're going to be from one moment to the next.

A shot rings out. JADE *falls to the ground, an alarm clock in her hand. The alarm goes off.* JADE *is dead. A pause.*

GIDEON, *wearing a towel, bounds down the steps.*

GIDEON: Jade! It came off! I saw Roberta running around the hallway swinging his axe, and it just *shrivelled*. Isn't it wonderful what fear can do? Jade? (GIDEON *looks around for* JADE. IRENE *comes in from the garden.*)

IRENE: I heard a shot.

They both see JADE's *body.* GIDEON *bends down and turns off the alarm.* SAMMY *comes down the steps.*

SAMMY: What happened?

GIDEON: It came off, and Jade's dead.

MAGGIE *comes down the steps, behind* SAMMY.

MAGGIE: I don't want to look. My stomach hurts.

GIDEON: She was just a kid. Beneath the feathers. It's all shit, man.

MAGGIE: And I have *such* a headache.

IRENE: I'll bet the bullet came from that window again.

MAGGIE: *So shut the window!*

IRENE: There's no need to shout.

MAGGIE: People are dropping like flies. I *want* to shout.

SAMMY *sits in a lotus position, near* JADE's *body, and begins to chant.*

SAMMY (*chanting*): OMMM ...

GIDEON: Somebody here is on a really bad trip.

MAGGIE: It's not me. O.K. I admit I once was very jealous of young girls. But then I had my eyes lifted ...

SAMMY: OMMM ...

IRENE (*looks at the others*): Somebody here ... (*Stops herself, then turns to the garden door.*) I was on my way to ... (*Starts to move toward door, but* MAGGIE *is standing in front of it, and she suddenly thinks better of it.*) I better get another blanket. (*Walks up the stairs.*)

MAGGIE: She thinks it was one of us.

GIDEON: Yeah. (*Starts up the stairs.*)

MAGGIE: Where are you going?

GIDEON: I'm still filled with plaster.

SAMMY: OMMM ...

GIDEON: I have to wash.

MAGGIE: I wish people would stay in one spot.

GIDEON: You do?

MAGGIE: Don't look at me that way! *You're* the one with the motive. You're the one who got stuck. (GIDEON *goes upstairs.*)

SAMMY: OMMM ...

MAGGIE: Is that all you can say?

SAMMY: OMMM . . .

MAGGIE: I know what that is. That's Hindu. You're a total religious nut, aren't you? It doesn't matter *what* religion.

SAMMY: OMMM . . .

MAGGIE: And religion, like sex, is the prime cause of murder.

SAMMY: OMMM . . .

MAGGIE: So it could easily be you.

SAMMY: OMMM . . .

MAGGIE: I'm going upstairs.

ROBERTA (*off, upstairs*): Hey, fellow, where the hell are you?

MAGGIE: It's not safe upstairs . . . It's not safe downstairs. It's not safe. (*Sits on steps.*)

SAMMY (*in a trance*): It's safe here, in my heart. It took a long time, but it's at rest. You know what we're going to do, years from now, our monastery? We're going to open our gates and walk into the world, and the world will pretty well have smashed itself up by then, and we're going to pick up the pieces. When it's all over, we'll come out and pick up the pieces. I see it, here in my heart, clearly. We'll walk about the land, setting things right again, and there will be mountains again and sunsets and rivers, there will be rivers, and hopes and plans and thoughts, and the days that follow will be rich with creativity and joy and wonder . . . (*Silence – then he holds his head.*) Sorry. (*Looks up.*) Was I someplace else?

MAGGIE: More or less.

SAMMY *rises and walks to the other side of the room.*

MAGGIE: Where you going?

SAMMY: Putting out the candles.

MAGGIE: Don't leave me.

SAMMY: I'm just over here. (SAMMY *starts to blow out the candles.* MAGGIE *follows him around.*)

MAGGIE: I figured it out. The pattern. They were *alone* when they were killed. Except for the killer. You can't leave me.

SAMMY: Honey, at this point, don't even trust *me*.

MAGGIE: I don't. I just don't want to be alone. I've never trusted anyone. I didn't trust my husbands, I didn't trust Rick . . . I just didn't want to be alone. I *need* people even though I don't like them.

SAMMY: You can trust in God.

MAGGIE: Yeah. Where'd that get *you*?

SAMMY: This far.

MAGGIE: Not interested. God is too conventional. Those old things don't work any more.

SAMMY: So what does?

MAGGIE: Pizzazz. (*A pause.*) A lot of smoke clouds. Glitter. All the wrong things. They work. (SAMMY *heads for the study door.*) Where you going?

SAMMY: To the john.

MAGGIE: You can't.

SAMMY: I *can't*?

MAGGIE: You can't leave me alone. You promised.

SAMMY: I didn't promise. (SAMMY *walks into the study.* MAGGIE *follows him.*)

MAGGIE: I'll go with you.

SAMMY: I'll just be half a minute. Relax.

MAGGIE: *How*? (SAMMY *opens the bathroom door.* MAGGIE *starts to follow him in.*)

SAMMY: What are you doing?

MAGGIE: You're not going to leave me alone.

SAMMY: Look, all I want is a nice, quiet piss.

MAGGIE: Well go ahead.

SAMMY: By myself. Some things you do by yourself. Just stand by the door. Right there. I'm only a few feet away.

MAGGIE: You're sure?

SAMMY: Yes. Think of something calm and soothing. O.K.? (*Brushes his hand across her forehead.*) Try – just for a minute – to be at peace. (*Closes the bathroom door.*)

Silence.

MAGGIE: I can't think of a single thing that's calm or soothing. Nothing! What do you mean, *peace*?

A shot rings out. MAGGIE *grabs her stomach. Her body weaves. Falters. Then steadies.*

MAGGIE: Oh my God! It missed! (*Feels her body.*) I *think* it missed. Of course it missed. You don't get shot and not feel something. A little sting maybe, but *something*. Hey – how about that? It fucking well missed! Sammy? Did you hear that? (MAGGIE *opens the bathroom door.* SAMMY *falls out. He is dead.*)

MAGGIE: Sammy! But it's not possible. Not in there. (*Looks in the bathroom.*) A window! (*Kneels, cradles* SAMMY'*s body in her arms.*) Well, Listen, kid, you're probably the best place, you know? (*Sings softly, rocking him back and forth.*)
'Oh today, we'll merry merry be
Oh today we'll merry merry be
Oh today we'll merry merry be . . .
(*She stops. She stares at the study door. She rises and goes to the door, looks out and can see the garden door. There is a clear avenue of escape. She tiptoes out the door to the living room, then starts to walk to the garden door, at an increasingly rapid pace. Finally she is running. Suddenly she stops cold, in mid-step.*) DAMN IT! (*Falls to her knees.*) Goddamn it! (*Searches the floor.*) Why can't they make a contact lens that will stay in? Come on, where the hell are you? This is no time to fall out. Jesus! Where are you? I'm not running into the police station wearing glasses. No way. Oh! Come on! Bastard! I've got to get out of here. I've got to look good for the morning papers. *Come on!* (*Her hand touches something.*) Gotcha! (*Stands up in triumph, holding a tiny lens on her finger.*) I'm in business!

A shot rings out. MAGGIE *stands for a moment in disbelief. Then she falls to the floor, dead.*

Silence.

The telephone rings. ROBERTA *appears at the top of the stairs, still holding the axe. He looks down into the living room. The telephone continues to ring.* ROBERTA *walks down into the living room, swings the axe and brings it crashing down upon the telephone wire. He severs the wire.*

Silence.

ROBERTA *throws the axe down on top of the dead phone. He goes to a chair and takes a pocket book from it. He goes to a mirror, looks into it, and adjusts his makeup. He takes a little pillbox hat from the closet and puts it on. He takes another look, makes sure he's proper, and then walks to the garden door. He opens the door.*

A shot rings out. ROBERTA *falls into the garden, dead.*

Silence.

IRENE *comes down the staircase. She looks around, very slowly. She carries a blanket. She is trembling. She enters the living room, stands a moment, then goes to the study. She looks at* SAMMY'*s body. She returns to the living room, and looks at* MAGGIE'*s body. She turns to the garden and looks at* ROBERTA'*s body. She drops the blanket to the floor.*

GIDEON *appears at the top of the stairs. He glances at the bodies beneath him.*

IRENE *and* GIDEON *stare at each other.*

GIDEON: Why?

IRENE: You tell me. (GIDEON *walks down the stairs.* IRENE *backs away.*)

GIDEON: It's all over.

IRENE: Is it?

GIDEON: Yes. I don't mind now.

IRENE: Mind what?

GIDEON: What's going to happen.

IRENE: What *is* going to happen?

GIDEON: You know. (*Pause.*) I'm waiting.

IRENE: Is there some way I can appeal to you?

GIDEON: What about?

IRENE: I have two children.

GIDEON: It doesn't mean anything.

(IRENE *begins to back away toward the garden door.* GIDEON *follows.*)

IRENE: They have no one to take care of them. Their father's in Asia. He'll be there for six months.

GIDEON: What does it matter?

IRENE: It matters! They need me.

GIDEON: Why talk?

IRENE: I didn't know that my husband would be away so much. But then I never planned to marry into the military. War – killing – is repellent to me. I went on peace marches. Does that surprise you? Before I met Barry . . .

GIDEON: There's nothing left to say.

IRENE: But then I fell in love. Please, I beg you . . .

GIDEON: I've made up my mind.

IRENE: I have two children . . .

GIDEON: And nothing can change it.

IRENE: And a husband I love . . .

GIDEON: It's all over.

IRENE: *NO!* (IRENE *runs from the room, into the garden.*)

GIDEON: Don't run away. I've made up my mind. It's over. *You have to kill me!*

A shot rings out. GIDEON *smiles. He falls to the floor, dead.*

Silence.

IRENE *walks back into the room. She looks at* GIDEON's *body.*

IRENE: It doesn't make sense. (*She bends down and touches* GIDEON's *body, then pulls at it.*) Gideon! Is this some kind of joke? (*Rises.*) I didn't do this. I didn't kill him. I didn't kill *any* of them. (*Looks at other bodies.*) Everything *has* to make sense. You know that. Think it through. (*Sits on the steps.*) I didn't do it. I know I didn't do it. (*Silence.*) Come on. Think. (*Silence.*) Right now, at this moment, I don't remember doing any of this. That's the clue. I don't remember. Oh, for heaven's sake, this is silly. I didn't do it. (*Silence.*) It's not silly. There is logic in everything. And there is always an answer. Just think it through. I've read case histories. A person's mind can be separated into sections. One can

block out the other. I've read about that, so it has to be true. Maybe there are two parts of me. Oh, that's nonsense. No it's not. It's *possible*. And this part doesn't remember the other one, the one that kills. But I didn't do it. I *had* to do it. There's no one else. They're all dead. Gosh, if I could only remember . . . if I could only remember holding a gun or pulling a trigger or *something*. The gun. There has to be a gun. Where did I put the gun? I don't *have* a gun. It couldn't have been me . . . (*Silence.*) I had reasons. Lots of reasons. Rick! He's always been the same. So wild and free. And sensual. My goodness! He attracted me. Now, that's upsetting, isn't it? It has to be. So – there's a part of me that could kill him. Well it did. Obviously, it did. *But it didn't.* And Clay was making very improper advances. He wanted to put me in a dirty film. Sure. That other part of me could do it. It had a reason. Nadine – well, there was *really* a split personality; she'd catch on to me in no time. So that other part of me killed Nadine. And Jade . . . that little girl flaunted her promiscuity. That other part of me didn't like that. See, there's a pattern. And Sammy, because he kept making fun of me, *this* me, whenever I wanted to go to the police. And Maggie, because she was so *loud*. That's reason enough. And Roberta – Roberta was just there, by that time, what did it matter? And Gideon because he was the *only one left*. It was easy. The veranda outside looks into all the rooms and I didn't have to be too cautious, everyone was so stoned and out of it . . . It was so easy. All those flower-pots on the veranda! Of course. What a perfect place to hide the gun. It all fits! It's all clear. It all has logic. It *was* me. I did it! I killed Rick, I killed Clay, I killed Nadine, I killed Jade, I killed Sammy, I killed Maggie, I killed Roberta, I killed Gideon . . . (*Rises, crying:*) Oh thank God! Thank God! *It makes sense!* It was me!

A shot rings out.

IRENE: Shit.

IRENE *falls to the ground, dead.*

Silence.

Curtain.